DEPRESSION AMERICA

DEPRESSION AMERICA

Volume 4

POLITICAL TENSIONS

GROLIER
EDUCATIONAL

About This book

The Great Depression is one of the most important periods of modern U.S. history. Images of breadlines and hungry families are as haunting today as they were at the time. Why did the crisis occur in the world's richest country, and how has it shaped the United States today? *Depression America* answers these questions and reveals a highly complex period in great detail. It describes the uplifting achievements of individuals, tells touching stories of community spirit, and illustrates a rich cultural life stretching from painting to movie-making.

Each of the six volumes covers a particular aspect of the period. The first traces the causes of the Depression through the preceding decades of U.S. history. The second examines the first term of Franklin D. Roosevelt and the New Deal he put in place to temper the effects of the crisis. The third volume studies how the Depression affected the lives of ordinary Americans. Volume 4 reveals the opposition FDR faced from both the political right and left, while Volume 5 explores the effect of the period on U.S. society and culture. The final volume places the Depression in the context of global extremism and the outbreak of World War II, the effects of which restored the United States to economic health.

Each book is split into chapters that explore their themes in depth. References within the text and in a See Also box at the end of each chapter point you to related articles elsewhere in the set, allowing you to further investigate topics of particular interest. There are also many special boxes throughout the set that highlight particular subjects in greater detail. They might provide a biography of an important person, examine the effect of a particular event, or give an eyewitness account of life in the Depression.

If you are not sure where to find a subject, look it up in the set index in each volume. The index covers all six books, so it will help you trace topics throughout the set. A glossary at the end of each book provides a brief explanation of important words and concepts, and a timeline gives a chronological account of key events of the period. The Further Reading list contains numerous books and useful web sites to allow you to do your own research.

Published 2001 by Grolier Educational
Sherman Turnpike
Danbury, Connecticut 06816

© 2001 Brown Partworks Limited

Set ISBN: 0-7172-5502-6
Volume ISBN: 0-7172-5506-9

Library of Congress Cataloging-in-Publication Data
Depression America
    p. cm.
    Includes indexes
    Contents: v. 1. Boom and bust – v. 2. Roosevelt's first term – v. 3. Countryside and city – v. 4. Political tensions – v. 5. U.S. society – v. 6. The war years and economic boom.
    ISBN 0-7172-5502-6 (set : alk. paper)
    1. United States–Economic conditions–1918-1945–Juvenile literature. 3. New Deal, 1933-1939–Juvenile literature. 4. Working class–United States–Juvenile literature. 5. United States–Social life and customs–1918-1945–Juvenile literature. [1. Depressions–1929. 2. New Deal, 1933-1939. 3. United States–History–1919-1933. 4. United States–History– 1933-1945. 5. United States–Economic conditions– 1918-1945.]

HC106.3 D44 2001
330.973'0916–dc21

00-046641

For information address the publisher:
Grolier Educational, Sherman Turnpike,
Danbury, Connecticut 06816

Printed and bound in Singapore

For Brown Partworks
Volume consultant:
Kenneth E. Hendrickson, Jr., Chair,
History Department, Midwestern State University
Managing editor: Tim Cooke
Editors: Claire Ellerton, Edward Horton, Christine Hatt, Lee Stacy
Designers: Sarah Williams, Lynne Ross
Picture research:
Becky Cox, Helen Simm, Daniela Marceddu
Indexer: Kay Ollerenshaw

CONTENTS

1

LEFT VS. RIGHT

The Great Depression took place against an international background of increasingly extreme political ideologies. Within the United States, too, the crisis presented a challenge to political traditions on both left and right.

Democracy as we know it today has developed in conjunction with industrial economies that make possible the creation of large amounts of individual or corporate wealth, as reflected in the rise in general living standards in the western democracies over the past 150 years. The relationship between politics and economies is complicated, however. There is a range of answers to certain basic questions, including whether state intervention in the economy is good or bad, whether employees should be able to band together to bargain for higher pay, and whether the state should support the unemployed, sick, and old. Are there times when the pursuit of profit can have harmful long-term consequences? By the 20th century the varied answers to these questions had become important political fault lines (see Volume 1, Chapter 1, "The United States, 1865–1914").

By the late 1920s the competing political outlooks were increasingly presented in terms of mutually exclusive confrontations: capitalism vs. communism, right vs. left, employers vs. workers, American tradition vs. foreign values, countryside vs. city, drys vs. wets, central government vs. individual rights. Clashes between competing systems had led to

Germany's answer to economic hardship: Fascist leader Adolf Hitler reviews Nazi troops after coming to power in 1933.

communist revolution in Russia in 1917 and the rise of fascism in Italy in the 1920s and Nazism in Germany later that same decade (see Volume 6, Chapter 1, "Economics and Political Extremism in Europe and Japan").

Within the United States the antagonisms had been graphically manifested at the end of the 19th century in a series of bloody strikes as great corporations sought to smash America's fledgling unions. In the 20th century the philosophical conflict had been manifested in attacks by liberal, progressive politicians on monopoly and the trusts in the first decade of the century; in isolationism and the raising of barriers to immigration in the early 1920s; in the Red

Scare of Attorney General Mitchell Palmer in 1919, in which "subversives" were rounded up and deported; and in the triumph for rural values represented by the enactment of Prohibition in 1920. Such actions were all signs of the wider philosophical struggle being waged for the heart of the nation.

1. COMPETING IDEOLOGIES

A broad caricature of U.S. society in the first part of the 20th century presents a picture of businessmen and capitalists on the right objecting to government regulation of the economy and communists and socialists on the left advocating the revolutionary overthrow of the system. The divisions between political outlooks were rarely clear-cut, however. For all the tension between them, the differences between left and right were not always black and white. Big business, represented by magnates like John D. Rockefeller (1839–1937) and Andrew Carnegie (1835–1918), supported laissez-faire economics, or allowing the market to operate without government involvement; but many of the same people supported so-called "welfare capitalism," acknowledging that they had an obligation to the social welfare of their employees and their families. And while in simplistic terms leftist policies generally favored equitable wealth distribution and power for the working class, the leading union of the early part of the century, the American Federation of Labor, also rejected the idea of government regulation in favor of what its leader, Samuel Gompers (1850–1924), called "voluntarism." While European unions had a record of agitating for general socialist reform, the AFL concentrated U.S. union activity only on improving pay and conditions.

THE AMERICAN TRADITION

A distinctly American philosophical conflict against which the Great Depression took place was that between individualism—the freedom and rights of the individual—and mutualism, a social approach based on the individual's obligations to his or her society. Both belonged to the traditions of "American" republican values. In the period since the Civil War, however, mutualism had come

increasingly under pressure. At a time of rapid industrialization and economic expansion, some people argued, the social considerations represented by mutualism were a constraint on the entrepreneurs and business leaders who drove economic expansion.

Mutualism vs. Individualism

Critics of mutualism took an approach called Social Darwinism, named for the 19th-century naturalist Charles Darwin, who developed a theory of evolution based on the survival of the most adaptable representatives of a species. Social Darwinism saw capitalist society as a world in which the strong prospered at the expense of the weak, who became poor. There was little point in trying to improve conditions for these "weak" members of society.

The mutualist tradition, on the other hand, underlay the emergence of the labor movement in the late 19th century and that of the agriculturally based Populist Party in the 1890s. Its greatest defeats came in strikes like that at Home-

Troops fire on strikers in Maryland during the railroad strike of 1877. Such confrontations were signs of a deeper conflict within U.S. society.

stead and in the failure of successive governments to take action against the monopolistic trusts that dominated U.S. business. The absorption of the Populist Party into the Democrats kept its influence alive among both Republicans and Democrats in the early years of the 20th century, the so-called Progressive Era, when politicians on both sides advocated social reform to address the worst excesses of capitalism. After the federal government had managed the economy during World War I (1914–1918), however, the 1920s brought a return to minimal government interference in the internal workings of the economy and minimal U.S. involvement in the wider world.

THE WORLD CONTEXT

The conflicts in American ideology were played out against an international backdrop of political

The patience and orderliness of this 1932 breadline characterized the wider U.S. reaction to Depression: Few dreamed of revolution.

extremism (see Volume 6, Chapter 2, "The Victory of Authoritarianism"). It is difficult to imagine just how anxious Americans were made by the failure of democracy elsewhere. Both fascism and communism were dubbed "un-American," as were those—often recent immigrants—who followed them. What particularly worried Americans, however, was the rise of communism in Russia.

The Russian Revolution in 1917 brought to power a Bolshevik government based on a one-party state, workers' councils, a centrally planned economy, and the elimination of private business. The revolution's leader, Lenin, and the man who took his place after his death in 1924, Joseph Stalin, advocated the spread of worker revolution throughout industrial nations.

The reaction against communism played a part in the emergence of right-wing extremism in Europe. In 1922 Benito Mussolini,

backed by black-shirted, street-fighting fascists, became dictator of Italy. Adolf Hitler, leader of the Nazis, a small political party of extreme right-wing views, became chancellor of Germany in 1933 and dictator in 1934.

For some Americans these European remedies to the desperate economic situation and the failure of liberal democracy to

address it were attractive; to others they were disturbing. The mass of Americans continued to follow the two main political parties, which stayed largely in the political middle ground. Herbert Hoover and the Republicans tended toward the right and Franklin D. Roosevelt and the Democrats toward the left, but both worked within a democratic, constitutional framework.

There was never a realistic challenge to democracy in the United States. Desperate times, however, did lead many Americans to sympathize with more extreme views. While some progressives and liberals warmed to communist and socialist activities, some "traditionalists" would find inspiration in Europe's fascism. A variety of homegrown populist movements that drew on elements from both ideologies would mobilize millions of Americans.

The communist alternative: Joseph Stalin's Soviet Union seemed to increase industrial production through economic planning.

2. THE ECONOMIC DEBATE

The stock-market crash of 1929, in the words of one historian, "jolted average Americans awake"; the financial collapse that followed it challenged prevailing political and economic wisdom. There had been crashes and depressions before—the most severe one in recent decades in 1897—but what was unprecedented about the Great Depression was its severity and length.

When the U.S. economy stopped growing, the results were disastrous for America and the world. With fewer people consuming, industrial production in 1930 fell by 28 percent; two years later it had fallen by more than half. By July 1932 the U.S. steel industry was functioning at only 12 percent of its full capacity, and the average American wage was 60 percent lower than it been in 1929.

With a high demand for cash at home American finance houses began demanding payment of their short-term foreign loans. Because

Adam Smith founded modern economics in 1776 with the publication of his book The Wealth of Nations.

currency values were pegged to gold and 40 percent of that gold was sitting in the United States, convertible currency was scarce and thus hindered world trade. The total volume of international trade dropped by almost two-thirds, from $68.6 billion in 1929 to $24.2 billion in 1933. Outside

of the Soviet Union, world industrial production dropped 36.2 percent by 1932. In 1933 one in four American workers was out of a job; a fifth of the world population was out of work.

ORTHODOX VS. RADICAL

In the United States left and right disagreed about both the causes of and solutions to the Depression. The worst economic crisis in U.S. history made more pronounced the contrast between orthodox and radical economics. In general, industrialists and business interests were in favor of orthodox economics, while labor and the left defended radical theories.

Orthodox economics had its roots in the classical economic theories of men like Adam Smith, David Ricardo, and Robert Malthus. They and their followers had argued since the 18th century that when left free of any attempts at state regulation, the economy would regulate itself in accordance with natural economic laws (see box). Classical economics was

Classical Economics

The classical economic theories originally developed in Europe by Adam Smith in the 18th century, and revised by such thinkers as David Ricardo and Thomas Malthus, are sometimes known as "laissez-faire" economics, from a French term meaning "let them do it." Classical theory assumes that an economy is controlled by what Smith refered to as "the invisible hand of the market." It argues that basic economic problems, such as unemployment, high inflation, or depression, can be solved by market forces alone. If unemployment is high, workers will accept lower wages and thus stimulate increased demand for labor until unemployment falls again. The role of

government in such an economy is simply to protect property rights and ensure the stability of the currency, as well as providing certain public services that private firms would not provide, such as education.

After being highly popular in 19th-century Europe and in early 20th-century America, laissez-faire economics was abandoned in favor of more interventionist policies such as Keynesianism, partly as a result of its inability to explain or solve the depression. When unemployment and inflation rose in the early 1980s, laissez-faire policies were again adopted by Ronald Reagan in the United States and Margaret Thatcher in Great Britain.

Karl Marx in 1860. Marx's theories underlay Bolshevik success in the 1917 Russian Revolution and terrified American politicians.

based on a belief that human nature is intimately tied to self-interest and material reward, and that attempts to redistribute income would destroy incentives to work and disrupt the economic order. These economists saw state intervention in the economy as a violation of natural liberty, though over time they had come to accept the necessity of some form of state role for purposes such as defense or taxation. While views on individual freedoms varied greatly within this school of thought, its proponents generally come from the right of the political spectrum.

RADICAL ECONOMICS

Opposed to orthodox economics were radical economics, which were usually based on leftist theory. In the political and economic sphere the term "radical" referred to the searching out of the root of a problem and facing up to its consequences; radicals claimed to simply be going to the root of injustice and destroying it. Radical economists like Karl Marx, the 19th-century founder of communism, believed that the market, left to itself, would lead to periods of mass unemployment, environmental degradation, the exploitation of labor, and social polarization between haves and have-nots.

Marxism challenged classical economics by advocating centrally planned economies, government-regulated production based on need rather than profit, and the promotion of collective ownership of property in place of the class system created by private ownership. Marx argued that workers were alienated from what they made by the industrial process. Although communists and socialists were the primary proponents of radical economics, the description has been applied to everything from decentralization and personal freedom to totalitarianism.

HOOVER'S ORTHODOXY

The Great Depression was the biggest economic crisis since Adam Smith had laid out the principles of modern capitalism in the 18th century. Both analysis of its causes and recipes for recovery gravitated toward the two dominant poles of economic theory. At its broadest the argument became one between leaving the economy to correct itself and using government policy to try to do so. In the early years of the Depression the approaches taken by Herbert Hoover and FDR would come to crystallize the differences between the two schools of thought.

Only months before the Wall Street Crash Herbert Hoover moved into the White House in a climate of optimism and prosperity (see Volume 1, Chapter 7, "Hoover: The Search for a Solution"). The postwar economy was booming, and the new president was a firm believer in the idea that the economy could take care of itself. "We in America today are nearer to the final triumph over poverty than ever before in the history of any land," he proclaimed as a Republican nominee in 1928. Considering himself a progressive Republican, he preached a "third way" in American public life. This "associationalism" had clear roots in the mutualist tradition, with its call for government to inspire cooperation between corporate business interests and voluntary civic groups.

Hoover saw associationalism as a way to reconcile commercial interests with a society of self-governing individuals: "Commercial business requires a concentration of responsibility. Self-government requires decentralization and many checks and balances to safeguard liberty. Our government to succeed in business would need to become in effect a despotism. There at once begins the destruction of self-government."

The role of the federal government, Hoover felt, should not be that of master problem-solver, but rather that of the occasional helping hand. He generally believed that a combination of new technology and scientific business principles could abolish poverty and bring about a humane social order. He considered the ups and downs of the economy, which economists had identified as a cycle of boom and bust, to be normal and thought that individuals should be responsible for their own actions and left free of government intervention in their economic affairs.

HOOVER AND BUSINESS

Hoover was vehemently pro-business (see Volume 5, Chapter 1, "Government, Industry, and Economic Policy"). By keeping taxes low and placing minimal restrictions on entrepreneurs, he thought, the wealth created at the top would inevitably trickle down to those at the bottom of the economic ladder. The new president believed in the efficiency of industry and wanted to emulate that efficiency in government. He was particularly influenced by the business management system of Frederick Taylor, as espoused in

Aristide Briand (left) and Frank Kellog (right) in Paris. With no means of enforcement, their antiwar pact proved meaningless.

his book *The Principles of Scientific Management* (1911) (see box, page 12). Taylorism was revolutionizing industry with its emphasis on greater managerial control over workers and their pace of production, its stress on standardized production processes, and its close accounting. While workers generally considered the process dehumanizing, managers and entrepreneurs praised the system's efficiency in generating profits. When Hoover took power in 1929, he appointed to low-level government positions hundreds of young professionals trained in Taylorism, statistics, and the social sciences. In keeping with his belief in the wealth-creating power of capitalism, he appointed six millionaires to his cabinet.

AFTER THE CRASH

The stock-market crash took both Republicans and Democrats by surprise. Hoover had been concerned about speculation and insider trading on the stock market and its potentially disastrous

effects, but publicly exuded optimism. His faith in the power of the economy to run itself made him believe that the crash was a temporary economic downturn, that prosperous times were "just around the corner." He attempted to convince the nation, in radio addresses and in talks around the country, that the nation's industrial base was sound.

Hoover's ideological outlook precluded the federal government from providing direct monetary

Taylor and Taylorism

Frederick Taylor, pictured around the turn of the century, believed that his reforms would improve life for workers: They often disagreed.

Frederick W. Taylor was born in Philadelphia in 1856. He excelled at school but was forced to abandon his studies after damaging his eyesight by studying in poor light. Instead, when his eyesight recovered, he became an apprentice patternmaker at an engineering plant, from where he moved to the Midvale Steel Company as a laborer. Taylor worked his way up to become chief engineer at the plant. A skilled inventor and national tennis doubles champion, Taylor increasingly focused on the problems of efficiency in the workplace. He realized that by closely studying the routines of workers—a discipline that became known as time management—it was possible to see where time was being wasted and eliminate the wastage. Were workbenches too far apart, for example, so that workers had to move more than was necessary?

For its critics, particularly in organized labor, such efficiency was inhuman, treating workers as parts of a machine rather than human beings who needed breaks or did not always work at the same pace. Carried to its extremes, the approach made working conditions almost unbearable. As employers soon discovered, however, Taylorism could make mass production far more efficient, as Taylor himself proved by designing and building a new machine shop at the Midvale plant based on the principles of "scientific management."

After 1890 Taylor launched a career as one of the first management consultants; in 1911 he published the influential study *The Principles of Scientific Management.* He continued to promote his system of management until his death in 1915. It was highly influential in the development of industrial practices in the first part of the 20th century.

relief to the the unemployed; this, he believed, was the job of private relief groups working at the community level (see Chapter 5, "Welfare"). "The sole function of government is to bring about a condition of affairs favorable to the beneficial development of private enterprise," he said. "Every time the government is forced to act, we lose something in self-reliance, character, and initiative." The president traveled the nation trying to inspire business and community groups to work together in providing relief and creating new jobs. He asked business leaders to keep up wages and prices to stimulate spending. "Depression can not be cured by legislative action or executive pronouncement," he told Congress in 1930. That same year unemployment reached 11 percent: Hoover reacted by setting up his Emergency Committees for Employment to coordinate the relief efforts of private charities.

Balancing the Budget

Hoover believed passionately in balancing the federal budget and keeping income taxes low. He continually vetoed congressional relief measures; when the administration did give out money, it was normally to big business and reflected the belief that only big business could revive the economy and create jobs. When presented with a giant public power project for the Tennessee River Valley, he rejected it in fear that cheap electricity would constitute undue competition for private power companies, even though as secretary of commerce in the 1920s he had advocated similar plans.

Hoover convinced the Federal Reserve Board to lower interest rates; entrepreneurs could borrow money more cheaply in order to invest in business expansion. Instead of taxing the wealthy, the president agreed to a national tax on manufactured goods. But with the purchasing power of most Americans decimated, there was no consumer market large enough to encourage businesses to expand. There were fewer manufactured goods to tax. Products remained on store shelves, and retailers sent fewer orders to factories.

Despite his belief in unregulated markets, however, Hoover approved the Smoot-Hawley Tariff Act of 1930. It imposed import duties of up to 50 percent on foreign imports to the United States. This set off a tariff war and deprived European exporters of access to U.S. markets, and thus dollars to pay off debts accrued in World War I; the Depression was in effect exported.

HOOVER'S NEW POLICY

As the depression continued and unemployment continued to rise, Hoover became more flexible and started agreeing to more federal aid. On January 22, 1932, he got Congress to approve the Reconstruction Finance Corporation (RFC). The agency loaned millions of dollars to railroads, business corporations, banks, and other institutions. In July the Emergency Relief Act extended aid to agriculture and financed public works projects at state and local levels. Also that summer Hoover agreed to $300 million in RFC loans to states that needed the money for welfare. He also had Congress authorize $500 million for public works projects like the Hoover Dam.

These moves were too little, too late. Unemployment had risen from 3 percent to 25 percent; more than 100,000 Americans had applied for jobs in the Soviet Union. Despite Hoover's attempts to stabilize the economy, average Americans perceived him as callous and cold-hearted. He became the personification of what was wrong with America.

One of the strongest blows to public confidence came with the repression of the Bonus Expeditionary Force by Douglas MacArthur in 1932. Against Hoover's instructions MacArthur sent in troops to attack World War I veterans who had marched to Washington to demand payment of a long-delayed service bonus. Furious with the soldier in private, Hoover had little choice but to back him in public (see box, page 21).

FDR'S VICTORY

For thousands of Americans it did not matter who the Democratic Party nominated in the 1932

A cartoon shows Hoover as the Statue of Liberty with its torch pointing downward, a suggestion that he was failing to uphold American values.

presidential elections. The next president could be anyone but Hoover. The theories of classical economics had failed completely. This was the nadir of the political right in the United States: Years would pass before it would return to national power.

Roosevelt's campaign offered Americans a "new deal"; vague as it was, the promise was enough for him to win and gain the Democrats overwhelming control in Congress (see Volume 2, Chapter 1, "The Election of 1932").

ROOSEVELT THE RADICAL?

Just as Hoover had brought to Washington a legion of young professionals, Roosevelt relied on associates from the academic world. What they had in common was their willingness to experiment with direct government

World War I veterans of the Bonus Army travel to Washington, D.C., in 1932. MacArthur and Hoover justified attacking them by claiming, falsely, that they were led by communists

intervention in the economy. While far from the left wing of radical economics, Roosevelt believed that a certain degree of intervention in the economic affairs of the nation was necessary.

Roosevelt and his aides were worried by economic disorder and believed in government regulation to end it; like the Progressives of the early century, they were opposed to business monopoly and generally supported the right of labor to organize and challenge business interests. Unlike many of their predecessors, they believed that poverty was not the result of moral failure, but generally the result of socioeconomic forces like unemployment or poor housing. Rather than blindly follow any one school of thought, however, the new administration was committed to experimentation. If a policy failed, it was dropped and a new one tried.

Roosevelt's first hundred days in office were a whirlwind of activity (see Volume 2, Chapter 2, "The First Hundred Days"). Through the National Recovery Administration Roosevelt sought cooperation among business, labor, and government to stabilize wages and prices. The Public Works Administration put hundreds of thousands of Americans to work on projects that improved the nation's infrastructure.

The Federal Deposit Insurance Corporation reformed the banking system by insuring bank deposits. The stock market was to be regulated by the Securities and Exchange Commission. The Agricultural Adjustment Administration used production controls and farm subsidies to protect U.S. farmers from the vagaries of the market. Relief agencies like the Civil Works Administration, the Federal Emergency Relief Administration, and the Civilian Conservation Corps were federal attempts to aid the unemployed (see Volume 2, Chapter 5, "Putting People to Work"). The new administration imposed taxes on large fortunes, but many observers on the left

considered that action to be more symbolic than a real attempt at wealth redistribution.

Such was probably the case. Roosevelt was no revolutionary. There were actually numerous precedents for federal involvement in the economy in the shape, for example, of grants to encourage road and railroad building in the 19th century or the management of the economy during World War I.

Despite the criticisms that each leveled against the other, there was also a considerable degree of continuity from Hoover to FDR. Hoover had launched public works

A Lurch to the Left?

Critics accused Roosevelt of steering the United States dangerously close to socialism. Such was not really the case, but there were numerous ways in which the administration seemed more left wing than it was. Not least was the high profile of Eleanor Roosevelt. While her husband was prepared to compromise for the sake of practical politics, the First Lady spoke out freely about reform issues that the right inevitably found socialist, particularly in regard to racial segregation. Roosevelt also introduced a large number of intellectuals to government, which was previously dominated by businessmen. The liberal academics who surrounded him could not fail but arouse the suspicion of the business community.

Star Al Jolson helps publicize the National Recovery Administration. The NRA codes were originally popular with bosses and labor alike.

projects like the Hoover Dam to create employment, and his administration had drafted most of the banking laws introduced by FDR. Hoover admitted that he would himself have signed virtually all of the New Deal legislation, while one of FDR's Brain Trust, Rexford Tugwell, acknowledged that much of that legislation drew on the measures Hoover belatedly adopted to fight the Depression.

REDISTRIBUTION OF WEALTH

Critics on the right bitterly attacked FDR's early attempts at intervening in the economy. Those on the left also criticized him for not doing more to redistribute wealth within U.S. society. In this, they argued, he betrayed all too clearly his fidelity to his privileged, upper-class origins. America's problems, such critics believed, derived partly from the fact that the top 36,000 families (0.01 percent of the population) controlled as much wealth as the 42 percent of families (11.5 million) at the bottom. In 1929 nearly two-thirds of the American population earned less than the minimum subsistence level of $1,500 a year. Although most Americans did become better off during the 1930s, the relative distribution of wealth remained broadly the same in 1940 as it had been in 1930.

In rural America—which was still home to one-fifth of the population in 1930—farmers earned about one-third of what nonfarm workers earned. The effect of all this was that many Americans did not wield the purchasing power necessary to buy products and stimulate the economy.

3. POLITICS AND LABOR

One area in which Roosevelt's administration had a significant effect was in labor law. Right-wing politicians and economists believed that it was important for the free running of the economy that businesses were protected from potentially ruinous strikes. On the extreme left wing, socialists believed in regulation of the economy in favor of the many rather than the few. A more center-left view was that workers should have the right to organize themselves against the power of business owners, and that an increase in working-class purchasing power would benefit the economy as a whole. So, in place of the unregulated market advocated by supporters of laissez-faire economics or the state ownership and economic control promoted by socialists, Roosevelt's New Deal advocated the "broker state," in which the government would facilitate a structure within which labor, business, and other social agents could engage in constructive dialogue.

The broker state created a climate in which labor unions, whose activities had been relatively restricted, could flourish. The 1930s brought numerous prolabor policies, though some were later overturned by the U.S. Supreme Court (see Chapter 2, "The Supreme Court"). In 1930 the Court upheld the Railway Labor Act, which banned employers' influencing workers' choice of bargaining representatives. With the Anti-Strikebreaker (Byrnes) Act it became illegal "to transport or aid in transporting strike-breakers in interstate or foreign

A sharecropper family and their home: FDR's critics accuse him of missing the opportunity to eradicate such grinding poverty.

commerce." The Public Contracts (Walsh-Healey) Act made government contracts subject to binding standards, including health safety requirements, child and convict labor rules, and a minimum wage. In 1931 the Davis-Bacon Act introduced standard wage rates for laborers employed by contractors and subcontractors for public construction projects. The following year the Anti-Injunction (Norris-La Guardia) Act banned federal injunctions in certain labor disputes. Section 7(a) of the

National Industrial Recovery Act guaranteed every employee's right to organize and bargain collectively through their union representatives without pressure or interference by employers.

In 1934 the United States joined the International Labour Organization (ILO), and the secretary of labor called the first-ever National Labor Legislation Conference to promote closer cooperation between the states and the federal government in developing a national labor legislation program; the conferences would last until 1955. In 1935 the National Labor Relations (Wagner) Act established the first national labor policy to protect workers' right to organize and elect representatives for collective bargaining. In 1938 further legislation tackled the problem of child labor.

Union leaders took advantage of a government attitude that was at times neutral and at times prolabor, and organized. One United Mine Workers' leaflet read, "The president wants you to join a union." Union membership grew by leaps and bounds. In 1930 there

were 3,632,000 union members; by 1945 there were 14,796,000 (see Chapter 6, "The Unionization of Labor"). The growth of activism rekindled an active leftist culture that had, since World War I, been almost dormant.

THE U.S. LEFT

By the start of the Great Depression the American left had lost some of its most charismatic leaders (see box, opposite). America's most celebrated socialist, five-time presidential candidate Eugene V. Debs, had died in 1926. Lithuanian-born anarchist and feminist Emma Goldman

FDR and Communism

Roosevelt was criticized for not being as passionate in denouncing communism as other politicians of the same period. Critics condemned him for giving diplomatic recognition to the Soviet Union and for not taking the communist threat seriously. They also said that the many New Deal agencies provided work for communists, and possibly even for Soviet spies.

In fact, FDR always said that communism was incompatible with American ideals of freedom and individualism. If he was not more anticommunist, it was partly because the American Communist Party had fewer than 80,000 members and little influence, and also because they were in broad sympathy with his policies, and he did not see them as a threat.

Lost Leaders of the Left

By the 1930s the American left had lost some of the charismatic figures who dominated the movement at its peak from the 1890s to the aftermath of World War I. Chief among them was Eugene Victor Debs, who had died in 1926; as leader of the Socialist Party Debs won 915,000 votes in the presidential election of 1920, despite then being in prison for sedition. His result in the 1912 election remains the high-water mark for the left in national politics in the United States.

Born in Indiana in 1855, Debs left home at age 14 to work on the railroad. He formed a local lodge of the Brotherhood of Locomotive Firemen in 1875 and later became national secretary. In 1893 he became president of the new American Railroad Union, in which position he organized the 1894 Pullman Strike in Chicago. The strike, one of the largest of the time, made Debs a national hate figure and saw him sentenced to six months in prison. There he read Marx and turned to socialism, and in 1901 he was involved in founding the Socialist Party of America. He was the party's

Eugene V. Debs captivates a meeting in 1912. An instinctive rather than intellectual socialist, Debs won support with his obvious sincerity.

candidate for president in 1900, 1904, 1908, 1912, and 1920. By the last he was in prison for sedition, having been jailed under the 1917 Espionage Act for his opposition for the war. Debs was released by order of President Harding in 1921, but his citizenship, which had been stripped, was not restored until 1976.

Russian-born Emma Goldman emigrated to the United States in 1885 and soon began espousing anarchism in a tireless campaign of public lectures. Her associate, Alexander Berkman, was jailed for attempting to assassinate industrialist Henry Clay Frick during the Homestead strike of 1892; Goldman spent a year in jail for inciting a riot in New York City in 1893. They were both arrested for obstructing the draft in 1917 and were deported to Russia two years later. There Goldman became disillusioned with the Soviet system she had previously supported, and in 1921 she moved to England.

William "Big Bill" Dudley Haywood (1869–1928) had, with Debs, founded the radical Industrial Workers of the World in 1905 and become its leader. In 1917 he was convicted of sedition; four years later, on bail during an appeal, he fled to Russia, where he worked for the revolutionary government until his death.

A contemporary cartoon shows FDR interrupting bosses of the CIO and AFL—who had come to blows at a union convention—at the time the CIO split from the larger union.

(1869–1940) had from 1908 to 1917 spoken out in support of anarchism and women's rights, but her antiwar stance led to her deportation to Russia in 1919.

The Industrial Workers of the World, the revolutionary industrial union that Debs founded with William D. Haywood and Daniel De Leon was, by 1930, at one-third of its original strength, with only 10,000 members, the so-called Wobblies. The IWW had failed in its goal to unite skilled and unskilled laborers to overthrow capitalism and rebuild society through socialism.

Unionism did offer a more radical option after the formation of the Committee for Industrial Organization in 1935. The committee's leaders broke away from the more conservative American Federation of Labor (AFL) to call for mass unions rather than the traditional craft-based unions, giving organized support to millions of unskilled workers. CIO leader John L. Lewis (1880–1969) donated $500,000 to Roosevelt's reelection campaign in 1936, a clear sign that the left appreciated the value of the government's attitude of neutrality if not support. In 1937 the CIO won a six-week sit-down strike at the General Motors plant in Flint, Michigan, partly because a number of key Democratic politicians, including FDR, were reluctant to use the police to evict the strikers.

After the strike at Flint more than 1.5 million workers joined unions in early 1937, most in unions affiliated to the CIO. Sit-down strikes became common. Shop stewards spoke for workers and instituted grievance procedures. In company towns voters elected Democratic officials to replace traditionalist Republicans.

Later in 1937 a new recession saw industrial production fall by up to 50 percent. Many workers were laid off. Meanwhile, the militancy of the CIO in a series of strikes was alienating employers and politicians alike, including FDR, who distanced himself from the union. The growth of the CIO slowed; later it rejoined the AFL, whose membership it had never been able to rival, to form the AFL-CIO. Rather than pursue radical ideology or major social change, union leaders focused mainly on achieving higher wages and better working conditions for their members. Some leftist historians regret this lost opportunity for the birth of a radical American worker ideology based on egalitarianism and class struggle.

Strikers set on a steelworker, in the black suit, as he crosses a picket line in Pennsylvania in 1937. Strikes remained potentially violent.

James Ford (right) of the Communist Party became the first black American to be nominated as vice president in 1932; with him is presidential hopeful William Foster.

The communist-led National Miners Union convinced black miners to strike with white miners in Pennsylvania and got striking white miners in Kentucky to desegregate the strike kitchen. The communists ran several African Americans for public office. Black support for communism was strengthened through the International Labor Defense's (ILD) campaign in support of the Scottsboro boys, nine young black men falsely convicted of raping two white women on a train in Alabama. The ILD gained the trust of the boys' families and thus part of the black community, and the case became an example of black and white Americans organizing and demonstrating together.

4. POLITICS AND RACE

While unionization and activism did not bring the widespread social and political change desired by radicals, it did cross racial lines and open new job opportunities to nonwhites. For both political and economic reasons many African Americans would find their home at the left of the political spectrum, in the Democratic Party or in more radical political options. Black Americans were hit especially hard by the Depression (see Volume 5, Chapter 2, "Equality for Some"); they were always among the first to be laid off. But while the economic, agricultural, and housing programs of the New Deal were not always equitable, many opened up areas previously closed to African Americans. New Deal writing projects involved black writers; black employees of the Works Project Administration (WPA) interviewed exslaves. A growing black working-class consciousness brought many African Americans into the labor movement. Asa Philip Randolph (1889–1979) had

led the Brotherhood of Sleeping Car Porters (BSCP) since 1925; after the Amended Railway Labor Act (1934) he achieved recognition for the union in a contract from the Pullman Company, and the BSCP became the first national union of black workers to join the American Federation of Labor (AFL).

The U.S. communist movement, named the Communist Party of the United States of America (CPUSA) in 1928, was attractive to many intellectuals in African American political and cultural life. Since American communists defended the establishment of a black republic in the South, some African Americans saw it as a complement to the Black Nationalist movement.

For black Americans who saw in capitalism a system founded on slavery and strengthened through racism the antiracist activities of American communism were also appealing. While liberal and progressive groups of the era often tolerated racial segregation, communists strongly opposed it.

5. BACKLASH FROM THE RIGHT

Roosevelt's policies brought him many enemies among America's wealthy (see Chapter 4, "The Right-wing Backlash"). Many on the right preferred not to utter his name, calling him "that man in the White House." While Roosevelt had originally planned to build an alliance joining all social and economic classes, conservatives were outraged at the growing power of government and labor unions. Many feared FDR's talk of confiscatory taxation and attacks on corporate monopolies.

THE AMERICAN RIGHT

By August of 1934 the American right was on the counterattack. The strongest opposition to FDR came from an alliance of conservative politicians and businessmen called the American Liberty League. In the congressional elections of 1934 the league backed candidates from both major parties who were opposed to FDR. Attacking the New Deal as socialistic, authoritarian, and unconstitutional, the league had the support of conservative Democrats like John W. Davis and the backing of some of America's wealthiest people, including John Raskob and the Dupont family.

The fundamental aim of the league was to protect private property. Its articles of incorporation stated: "The particular business and objects of the Society shall be to defend and uphold the Constitution of the United States and to gather and disseminate information that (1) will teach the necessity of respect for the rights of persons and property as fundamental to every successful form of government and (2) will teach the duty of government to encourage and protect individual and group initiative and enterprise, to foster

the right to work, earn, save and acquire property, and to preserve the ownership and lawful use of property when acquired."

Property Rights

The league made little distinction between property rights and human rights. According to one of its widely circulated pamphlets, written by its president Jouett Shouse: "The two so-called cate-

Nazis of the German-American Bund parade down a New York street in 1938. U.S. sympathies with fascism had peaked by 1936.

gories of rights are inseparable in any society short of Utopia or absolute communism. To protect a man's so-called human rights and strip him of his property rights would be to issue him a fishing license and them prohibit him from baiting his hook.... Government disregard for property rights soon leads to disregard for other rights. A bureaucracy or despotism that robs citizens of their property does not like to be haunted by its victims."

The league created largely unsuccessful alternative political movements like the Southern Committee to Uphold the Constitution and the Farmers' Independence Council. Attempts to rally grass-roots Democratic opposition to the New Deal also failed; the league briefly supported Democratic Georgia governor Eugene Talmadge's presidential

Businessman Henry Ford, center, proudly accepts the Order of the German Eagle, the Nazis' highest award to foreigners.

MacArthur and the Right

One of the most conspciuous supporters of the American right was Army chief of staff General Douglas MacArthur (1880– 1964). MacArthur was a four-star general with a four-star military record that included action in the occupation of Vera Cruz in Mexico in 1914, on the Western Front in World War I, and as superintendent of the U.S. Military Academy at West Point. On becoming chief of staff in 1930, MacArthur at once faced the problems caused by the Depression and spent much of his energy maintaining Army strength in the face of spending cutbacks. He also played an important role in the administration of the Civilian Conservation Corps (CCC).

To many observers MacArthur was independent minded and willful. He defied Herbert Hoover in June 1932 when he sent federal troops to attack the Bonus Army in Washington, D.C., against the orders of the president. Believing that the veterans were communists, MacArthur declared "I will not permit my men to bivouac under the guns of traitors." He sent in troops to tear-gas and set fire to the protestors' camp. Although he felt obliged to support MacArthur in public, Hoover branded him one of the two most dangerous men in America, along with radical Louisiana senator Huey Long.

MacArthur retired from the Army in 1937 but returned when the United States entered World War II as an Allied commander in the Pacific. He led the campaign to recapture the Philippines and received the Japanese surrender in 1945. He commanded the U.S. occupation of Japan from 1945 to 1951 and went on to lead U.S. forces in the Korean War in 1950. Once again he defied the will of the president, ignoring Harry S. Truman's desire to fight a limited war. This time he did not get away with his insubordination: The president relieved MacArthur of his command.

---

aspirations in 1936, but the move brought little new support.

One of the league's main problems was that it lacked a clear leader. Ex-president Hoover was a vociferous New Deal critic but refused to join the league, saying, "As to liberty of the Wall Street model, I am not for it." The league convinced the 1928 Democratic presidential candidate, former New York governor Alfred E. Smith, to support its efforts, but Smith's extremist views and bitter comments at a fund-raiser in January 1936 tarnished both his and the league's reputation.

An American Coup?

There were accusations that the league was willing to work outside of the law when it wished. According to testimony by retired U.S. Marine Corps Major-General Smedley Darlington Butler before Congress's Special Committee to Investigate Nazi Propaganda Activities in the United States, he was approached by league representative Gerald MacGuire in 1933. MacGuire wanted him to lead 500,000 veterans to march on Washington and take Roosevelt captive. Mac-Guire allegedly claimed that Al Smith, General Douglas Mac-Arthur, General Hugh Johnson (head of Roosevelt's National Recovery Administration), and several other generals and admirals were aware of the planned coup attempt. MacGuire died before the investigation was through; the allegations were largely dismissed by the press, and the issue was forgotten. When FDR won the election of 1936, the league passed into oblivion.

MacArthur (left) directs the attack on the Bonus Army in Washington, D.C., in June 1932.

Dr. Francis Townsend, seated, and the board of directors of his campaign to provide old-age pensions for all Americans.

THE RIGHT AND HITLER

Just as international communism inspired many on the American left, many on the right were initially encouraged by right-wing developments in Europe. In Germany the severe depression sparked widespread support among Germans for the extremist politics of Adolf Hitler and the Nazi Party. While similar parties created in the U.S. were of little importance, Americans like industrialist Henry Ford (1863–1947) shared Hitler's anti-Semitism and the view that Jewish bankers were behind many of the world's problems. Ford's anti-Jewish sentiments led him to write his pamphlet *The International Jew: The World's Foremost Problem.* Hitler awarded Ford the Order of the German Eagle, Nazism's highest civilian honor, in 1938.

Just as American communists were largely unaware of the human rights abuses and political re-pression carried out by Stalin in the Soviet Union, fascist sympathizers were unaware of the genocidal consequences fascism would bring. Anti-Semitism notwithstanding, what they saw during the Depression was a Germany that, of all the Western states, was the only one to eliminate unemployment.

6. POPULIST PRESSURE

By the eve of the 1936 elections dissatisfaction with the extent of FDR's reforms had seen the rise of a number of populist leaders whose demagoguery occasionally resembled that of Europe's extremist leaders. Huey Long of Louisiana championed a "Share Our Wealth" campaign that argued for a redistribution of wealth and the development of the public sector (see Chapter 3, "Huey Long"). Catholic priest Father Charles Coughlin used radio broadcasts to address up to 40 million Americans. Although he originally supported FDR, he soon distanced himself from the administration and formed the National Union for Social Justice. The organization opposed the New Deal and called for the nationalization of banks, utilities, and natural resources. Coughlin's broadcasts and *Social Justice* magazine became increasingly anti-Semitic and praised Mussolini and Hitler.

A third populist, Dr. Francis E. Townsend, proposed in 1933 the Townsend Plan, which would provide pensions for all Americans over 60 by imposing a national 2 percent sales tax. By 1936 there were some two million members in Townsend Clubs all over the country, formed to lobby Congress for enactment of the plan.

THE UNION PARTY

By the election of 1936 numerous changes had weakened the appeal of the populists. The movement lacked a clear leader. Huey Long's assassination left the Share-Our-Wealth movement without its presidential hopeful. Reverend. Gerald L. K. Smith, a fiery orator from the Disciples of Christ Church, led Long's followers for a short time but was later denounced for fascist sympathies. The Townsendites remained active, though all hopes of the Townsend plan becoming law were dashed by the passage of the Social Security Act on August 14, 1935.

The push for an alternative to mainstream politics saw the three populist movements combine in 1936 to form the Union Party. Because none of its more charismatic figures wanted to run, the party chose North Dakota's Republican congressman William Lemke as its presidential candidate. He polled fewer than 900,000 votes. The Union Party was disbanded four days after FDR's landslide victory, Father Coughlin went off the air for a time, and the Townsend movement slowly disintegrated.

Keynes also argued that states had a role in it. According to him, for example, governments faced with a depression should offset private spending decreases with increases in public sector spending—even if it meant an unbalanced budget. Governments could control money supply, spend money, and adjust taxes to soften the "boom and bust" cycles criticized by radical economists. Keynesian thought would replace laissez-faire economics as mainstream American economic policy until the 1980s. Keynesian thought was also vital to the emergence of social democracy in Europe after World War II, in which governments nationalized certain key industries and instituted welfare states but preserved the framework of a free market economy.

British economist J. M. Keynes, whose theories became the accepted economic orthodoxy in the West in the mid–20th century.

While belonging to neither left nor right, these movements contained elements of both. Many Americans saw benefits in socialism; others believed that Hitler and Mussolini were good for their countries. Both approaches accepted the need for a more active role for government in the economy, and this was strongly supported by the populist movement. It would disintegrate, but not without having pushed FDR to the left and causing him to extend federal intervention in the social and economic evolution of the country.

7. A NEW ECONOMIC THEORY

That Roosevelt was pushed to the left is indicative of a larger trend within the conflict between ortho-dox and radical economics. The Great Depression proved both orthodox and radical economics wrong. The failures of capitalism did not, as Marx had predicted, bring about a revolution of the working class. Nor did capitalism prove entirely self-regulatory. Instead, a fusion of the two systems brought a trend toward greater government regulation to correct certain abuses within capitalism. The so-called mixed economy pioneered during the Depression had a huge influence.

This new view of capitalism was reflected in the views of British economist John Maynard Keynes. In 1936 Keynes published his *General Theory of Employment, Interest and Money*. He argued that a mature capitalist economy was not, as orthodox economists had argued, self-correcting; it would stagnate and break down without a certain level of state intervention. While supporting the free market,

THE SUPREME COURT

One of the chief challenges to the New Deal in the mid-1930s came from the U.S. Supreme Court, which ruled key legislation unconstitutional. Roosevelt's plan to create a more liberal court gave ammunition to his conservative opponents, who accused him of bending the rules of the Constitution.

The United States had a tradition of a certain amount of government involvement in business regulation, the provision of welfare for the poor, and monitoring the conditions of workers. Franklin Roosevelt's inauguration in 1933 and the New Deal that followed it took the degree of intervention to a new level (see Volume 2, Chapter 2, "The First Hundred Days"). The American public, by and large, accepted that intervention in the economy was necessary for the government to bring about economic recovery.

Roosevelt's ambitious law-making program faced challenges, however, from conservatives and supporters of free-market economics (see Chapter 4, "The Right-Wing Backlash"). The conflict echoed that between the traditions of mutualism and individualism at the end of the 19th century (see Chapter 1, "Left vs. Right" and Volume 1, Chapter 1, "The United States, 1865–1914").

Roosevelt, part of the executive branch of the government, had a Democratic majority in the second branch, the legislature. Opponents

of his policies put their hope in the third branch, the judiciary in the shape of the U.S. Supreme Court. Since 1803 it had been the Court's role to review the constitutionality of laws passed by Congress and state legislatures. It challenged a number of measures, and Roosevelt came to see it as an unnecessary

Pictured in 1930 with Attorney General Mitchel (far left) are (left to right) U.S. Supreme Court justices Stone, Sutherland, Holmes, Hughes, Van Devanter, Brandeis, Butler, and Roberts.

John Marshall

The fourth chief justice of the United States, John Marshall (1755–1835), played a vital part in establishing the role of the U.S. Supreme Court in government. Prior to his appointment the court was largely ineffectual. Marshall's decisions set the precedent for judicial review of Congressional acts and thus turned the court into a powerful institution in American life.

Marshall was admitted to the bar in 1780. He moved to Richmond, Virginia, two years later and established himself as a leading lawyer in the state. In 1799 he was elected to the House of Representatives, and a year later he was made secretary of state by President John Adams. In 1801 he was appointed chief justice of the United States, a position he held until his death.

John Marshall was chief justice of the U.S. Supreme Court from 1801 until his death in Philadelphia on July 6, 1835. According to tradition, the Liberty Bell cracked while ringing at his funeral.

hindrance to his urgent reforms. To overcome the problem, Roosevelt resolved to alter the structure of the U.S. Supreme Court.

1. THE COURT AND THE U.S. CONSTITUTION

American democracy is based partly on the premise that tyranny can be avoided by separating the powers of government among different branches. The Constitution established three branches, each of which can act as a check on the others. Although it has at times paralyzed the workings of government or thwarted the expressed desires of the public, the system has never been seriously challenged. The three branches of the federal government are the executive, the actual governing body; the legislature, the law-making body, which includes Senate and House; and the judiciary, in the form of the Supreme Court and other federal courts.

In May 1922, after a 121-year interval, members of the U.S. Supreme Court take their places during the rededication of the original Supreme Court building in Philadelphia. The building had housed the first Supreme Court of the United States. True to the Supreme Court's respect for tradition, the justices of the 1922 court sat in the original chairs.

Appointing Justices

Supreme Court justices are appointed by the president and hold their place on the court for as long as they maintain, in the words of the Constitution, "good behavior." This indefinite period frees the judges from political pressure from either the Congress or the vested interests of litigants. They do not have to compromise their integrity in order to keep their place on the court. When a justice dies or is deemed unworthy of the task, the president appoints a new member, who must be approved by the Senate. Presidents who appoint justices have to make their selections very carefully, since the ideology of the justice could affect the court for years to come. During his presidency Roosevelt appointed nine justices.

In the early republic the judiciary had been by far the weakest of the government's three branches. In the 1803 case of *Marbury v. Madison*, however, Justice John Marshall (see box, page 25) declared part of the Judiciary Act of 1789 unconstitutional. Marshall's decision greatly strengthened the position of the court in the government.

Power of Judicial Review

Marbury v. Madison established that, if a law passed by Congress conflicts with the Constitution, the Supreme Court must base its decision on the Constitution. This ruling established the Court's power of judicial review, or its authority to declare laws unconstitutional. The Supreme Court exercised the prerogative only once more before the Civil War. In *Dred Scott v. Sanford*, 1857 it ruled that no African American could be a citizen or claim legal rights and that Congress had no power to prohibit slavery. The principle of judicial review made the judiciary a more or less equal

Chief Justice William Howard Taft (third from left) and associate justices of the U.S. Supreme Court examine a model of the Court's proposed new home in Washington, D.C., in 1929.

Judicial Traditions

Over the centuries numerous traditions have been adopted by the United States Supreme Court. They are still followed today.
• Twenty quill pens are set up on the counsel tables each day the court is in session.
• When the justices enter a room , they shake hands with each of their colleagues. This practice was meant to remind the court members that, notwithstanding their differences, they were all united in the same purpose. The so-called "judicial handshake" was introduced by Justice Melvin Fuller around the start of the 20th century.
• When the court begins a session, the court marshal cries out: "The Honorable, the Chief Justice and the Associate Justices of the Supreme Court of the United States. Oyez! Oyez! Oyez! All persons having business before the Honorable the Supreme Court of the United States are admonished to draw near and give their attention, for the Court is now sitting. God save the United States and this Honorable Court."

• The seating arrangement of the justices denotes their seniority. The chief justice sits in the center, and the justices align themselves in order of seniority from right to left; the most junior justice takes the last seat to the far left of the chief justice.
• Most cases reaching the U.S. Supreme Court involve a review of a previous decision made by the lower courts. The session in these cases is composed of justices and attorneys only. No jury or witnesses are present. Attorneys are allowed 30 minutes on each side to argue their case, after which the court retires to consider its verdict. When addressing the court, attorneys stand at the lectern in the center of the courtroom.
• The courtroom is lined on the left and right by rows of red benches. The press is seated on the left side of the courtroom, while the red benches on the right are taken up by guests of the justices. In front of these benches are a number of black chairs that are occupied by important visitors and officers of the court.

partner with the executive and legislative branches when it came to decision making.

Judicial Activism
After the Civil War the Supreme Court entered a phase of what observers called judicial activism. During this period the Court made decisions that tended to minimize state intervention in business. The Court advanced the doctrine of "substantive due process," based on the idea that certain state legislation denied "due process of law" under the Fourteenth Amendment. It struck down laws that protected workers,

A contemporary photograph of the U.S. Supreme Court building in Washington, D.C.

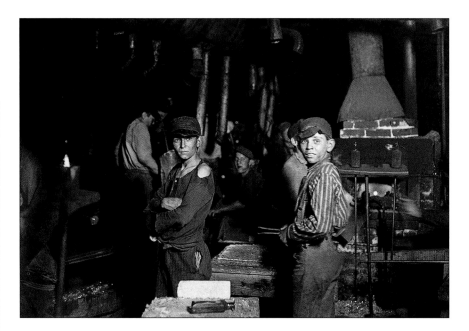

Child workers in a glassworks in Indiana at midnight. After the Civil War the judiciary agreed that the Fourteenth Amendment should be interpreted in favor of corporations, not the workers, and canceled laws against, among other things, child labor. In 1938 Roosevelt signed the Fair Labor Standards Act, abolishing child labor in some industries.

Civilian Conservation Corps, the Farm Credit Administration, the Federal Emergency Relief Administration, the Tennessee Valley Authority, and the National Recovery Administration (NRA).

including minimum wage laws and laws against child labor. Critics of this stance, including Justice Oliver Wendell Holmes, Jr., (served 1902–1932), argued that this interpretation of the amendment and decisions based on it were not based on the Constitution but on laissez-faire economic principles. The Court went on to prevent the adoption of a federal income tax until 1913 and frustrate federal efforts to prosecute industrial trusts and monopolies.

For a business to be subject to state regulation, the Court ruled in 1877, it must be "Clothed (or Affected) with a Public Interest." The term describes businesses that are either closely related to the public good, such as the public utilities, or that owe their existence to some government grant. In *Nebbia v. New York* in 1934 the Supreme Court finally allowed states authority to fix prices after half a century.

2. ROOSEVELT AND THE SUPREME COURT
In his first term Roosevelt's program included creating foreign policy, removing the country from the gold standard, and passing major legislation through Congress. The legislation included banking reform and the establishment of the Agricultural Adjustment Administration (AAA), the

NRA AND NIRA LEGISLATION
The National Recovery Administration aimed to balance each sector of the economy by regulating wages, prices, work

Lochner v. New York, 1905

The *Lochner v. New York* case of 1905 was pivotal to the idea that the government should not be allowed to interfere with companies or employees when they contract for work, which includes contracting for working hours. The decision in the case reflected the view, based on the court's interpretation of the Fourteenth Amendment, that government should control business and industry as little as possible. The case revolved around a New York State wage-and-hour law that limited bakers to a 60-hour working week. Joseph Lochner, a bakery owner, forced his employees to work more than 60 hours per week, thereby breaking the state law. He was convicted of the crime, but his lawyers challenged the decision. They maintained that the wage-and-hour law interfered with "liberty of contract," that is, it infringed the right to personal liberties and due process, thereby interfering with provisions of employment. The Supreme Court then overturned the decision, declaring the law unconstitutional and arguing that the state did not have the power to interfere with personal affairs of employment. It was not until much later, when Roosevelt began to introduce New Deal legislation, that the justices came under pressure to reexamine their decision and finally overturned the Lochner case. Up to that time their attitude on employment law had favored very limited government regulation.

A Home for the Court

When it was first created, the Supreme Court struggled to find a permanent place of practice. It met in various locations from the Exchange Building in New York City and the new Capitol in Philadelphia in 1790 to the final seat of government at Washington, D.C., in 1800. In Washington it still had no real permanent home and moved around a variety of locations, from taverns to committee rooms. Finally, on February 10, 1810, it moved into a new chamber, now known as the Capitol Building, designed and built specifically for the court by architect Henry Latrobe (1764–1820). Contemporaries described the chambers as "dark, damp, and dingy."

During the War of 1812 the Supreme Court was forced to vacate its chambers on Capitol Hill. The British had taken over and burned the Capitol, leaving the members of the court to find shelter for its work in rented houses nearby.

In 1860 the Supreme Court moved from the small, dimly lit room it then occupied into a first-floor chamber where the Senate had formerly held its sessions. Although this was meant as a temporary measure, the court remained there for the next 75 years. The larger room allowed for greater public attendance, and as a result, many people crowded onto the balcony to watch the proceedings. However, newspapers and politicians soon began to complain that this public attendance was having a negative effect on the court. The pressure of public examination, they argued, made it more difficult for the justices to remain unbiased.

In 1929 Chief Justice William Howard Taft, former president of the United States, persuaded Congress to provide the Supreme Court with an independent location. This would finally separate the court from the House and the Senate. In 1932 construction began on a new courthouse in Washington, which was completed in 1935. The Supreme Court now had its own place of residence, reflecting its equal and authoritative status as the third branch of the United States government.

---

hours, and competition. It was intended to act as a stabilizing force to prevent further economic instability, thereby promoting the growth needed to pull the country out of the Depression (see Volume 2, Chapter 5, "Putting People to Work"). The National Industrial Recovery Act (NIRA) provided the regulatory legislation that underscored much of the NRA's work. Business, labor, and government were to keep competition to a minimum by fixing prices and wages at an agreed level.

The justices take their seats in the Supreme Court early in the 20th century, when some observers began to argue against the presence of the public at hearings and for a specially built courthouse.

NIRA Ruled Unconstitutional
In 1935, in *Schechter Poultry v. United States*, the Supreme Court ruled NIRA to be unconstitutional (see Volume 4, Chapter 6, "The Unionization of Labor"). The case involved the Schechter brothers,

who ran a Brooklyn kosher-poultry business, and the metropolitan New York "Code of Fair Competition for the Live Poultry Industry," established under the provisions of NRA. The Schechters were indicted and

Carter v. Carter Coal Company, 1926

In *Carter v. Carter Coal Company* the court ruled as unconstitutional the Guffey Coal Act, which regulated wages, hours, and prices in the coal industry. It based its decision on the grounds that coal production did not fall under interstate commerce laws and that the act made an unconstitutional delegation of legislative power. Seven states had presented arguments that the problems of the coal industry could not be solved by independent state action, but the Court's decision effectively invalidated federal intervention.

Originally appointed chief justice by President Herbert Hoover in 1930, Charles Evans Hughes held the position throughout the Depression era. Hughes positioned himself with the more conservative justices in 1935 and 1936 but shifted toward the court's liberal wing after 1937, when a narrow minority of justices supported state minimum wage laws, the National Labor Relations Act, and the Social Security Act.

convicted in a federal district court on 19 counts for violation of NRA "fair practice" regulations, as well as for the sale of diseased poultry. When the Schechters appealed to the Supreme Court on May 27, 1935, it unanimously ruled NIRA to be unconstitutional. The Court's decision argued that the government was using law-making powers that, under the Constitution, it did not have. Codes, it declared, could not regulate activities that only indirectly affected commerce among states. Chief Justice Charles Hughes (1862–1948) wrote an opinion, or view, on the case warning the government that "Extraordinary [economic] conditions do not create or enlarge constitutional power.... Such assertions of extraconstitutional authority were anticipated and precluded by the explicit terms of the Tenth Amendment— The powers not delegated to the United States by the Constitution, nor prohibited by it to the States, are reserved to the States respectively, or to the people." The decision was a major blow to the president's entire New Deal program and underlined the ability of the Supreme Court to block reform legislation.

WORKERS' RIGHTS

Intrinsically linked to the question of federal regulation of business and industry was the issue of workers' rights. It was becoming increasingly apparent that legislation was needed if the conditions of labor were to be improved. However, the Supreme Court had shown no bias in favor of labor. Indeed, it often seemed to be working actively against the workers and for the corporations.

Labor relations in the United States improved when unions became more acceptable to employers. After the passage in 1935 of the National Labor Relations Act (NLRA), also known as the Wagner Act, unions became more widely accepted. The act established the National Labor Relations Board (NLRB) and required employers to accept a union as a

"Hot Oil," 1935

The *Panama Refining Company v. Ryan* case of 1935 tested the right Congress gave the president to "prohibit the transportation of interstate and foreign commerce" of oil produced or withdrawn from storage in excess of the amount permitted to be produced by the state from which it was shipped. The Supreme Court invalidated this provision by arguing that Congress had delegated essential legislative power to the president. Congress afterward passed an act that avoided the broad delegation of power but still regulated oil shipment.

West Coast Hotel v. Parrish, 1937

When she was fired from the Cascadian Hotel, Wenatchee, Washington, chambermaid Elsie Parrish asked for $216.19 in back pay, which she was owed according to a Washington State minimum wage law enacted in 1913. She was offered only $17 and filed suit for the full amount. The Cascadian Hotel's parent company, the West Coast Hotel Corporation, challenged the constitutionality of the Washington law. The Supreme Court voted to uphold the minimum wage legislation. The verdict overturned the same court's ruling the previous year that state minimum wage laws were unconstitutional (*Morehead v. New York ex rel. Tipaldo*, 1936). The decision reflected a general change in the court's attitude to New Deal legislation.

bargaining representative if chosen by a majority of employees.

The unions reinforced their bargaining power in different ways, including staging sit-down strikes. The sit-down strike was introduced into the United States from Europe in 1936 (see Volume 4, Chapter 6, "The Unionization of Labor"). It was used by the United Automobile Workers and other industrial unions. Labor leaders were quick to realize the potential value of this type of strike, in which workers took possession of a plant rather than picketing outside it. It was, as far as their advisers could tell, not only legal but also "the most effective and least costly way" for workers to protect their right to their jobs. However, in *National Labor Relations Board v. Fansteel Metallurgical Corporation* the Supreme Court ruled the sit-down strike illegal (see box, page 32), more or less putting an end to it as a means of protest.

The Schechter brothers celebrating the outcome of their case involving the live poultry code, in which the Court virtually crushed the NRA.

AAA DECLARED UNCONSTITUTIONAL

The Agricultural Adjustment Act (AAA) was introduced by Congress in 1933 in an attempt to stabilize the agricultural market (see Volume 3, Chapter 2, "Shadow over the Countryside"). Roosevelt introduced the bill to "relieve the existing agricultural emergency by increasing agricul-

tural purchasing power." This meant that farmers were allowed to receive subsidies from the government in exchange for reducing the amount of land they used for cultivation. By reducing farm surpluses, it was thought, prices would rise, and farm income would increase. Included in the statute was a provision to give the secretary of agriculture extensive authority to reduce productive acreage and to impose marketing quotas on farmers. Congress imposed a "processing tax" on the first processor of agricultural commodities to fund the subsidies promised to the farmers. After the AAA had been in operation for three years, however, the Supreme Court declared it unconstitutional in *United States v. Butler* (see Volume 3, Chapter 6, "Continuing Plight of the Farmer"). The court ruled that the taxation of agriculture processors was not within the jurisdiction of Congress; it was a function belonging to the individual states. The Court concluded that the AAA sought to regulate

Associate Justice James Clark McReynolds on the golf course. One of the most conservative justices, McReynolds was one of four known as the "Battalion of Death"—the others were Butler, Van Devanter, and Sutherland—who were all extremely hostile to almost any increase in federal power over industry and business.

agricultural development, which was a misappropriation of power by the executive and a violation of the Tenth Amendment.

FRAZIER-LEMKE ACT RULED UNCONSTITUTIONAL

After enacting the AAA in 1933, Congress, seeking to help farmers threatened with bankruptcy, had enacted the Frazier-Lemke Act, adding Section 75 to the Bankruptcy Act. The amendment provided temporary relief from bankruptcy for farmers who were unable to pay their creditors and lost their homes. The amendment allowed farmers to buy back their property, with title and right of possession, at its appraised value. Should the creditors refuse, the farmer could stay bankruptcy proceedings for up to five years, remaining in possession of the property. Should his financial situation improve in that time, he would be able to purchase the property without question.

Again, a unanimous Supreme Court came down on the side of corporate advantage. It ruled the act unconstitutional, declaring that the taking of property without compensation was a direct contravention of the Fifth Amendment. Justice Louis Brandeis (1856–1941) wrote that "however great the nation's need, private property shall not be thus taken even for a wholly public purpose without just compensation."

MINNESOTA MORATORIUM

Not all Supreme Court decisions went against the government. The height of the Depression saw not only farmers but many ordinary families unable to pay their mortgages. Under long-established laws mortgage holders had a right to foreclose on the mortgage, or take the property. This led to a plea to legislators for some kind of mortgage relief. In 1933 in Minnesota and some other states so-called mortgage moratorium acts were created.

The acts were immediately attacked on constitutional grounds (*Home Building and Loan Association v. Blaisdell*, 1934). Opponents argued that the moratorium acts

NLRB v. Fansteel Metallurgical Corporation, 1939

Early in 1937 police removed discharged workers staging a sit-down strike in a factory of the Fansteel Metallurgical Corporation in Chicago. The National Labor Relations Board ordered the reinstatement of the workers. The Circuit Court of Appeals refused to enforce the order, however, and the case came before the Supreme Court. On February 27, 1939, the court declared the sit-down strike to be "illegal in its inception and prosecution...without a shadow of legal right." The employers, on the other hand, had the right to "discharge the wrongdoers from its employ." The decision effectively ended the use of the sit-down strike in labor disputes.

Cartoonist Clifford Berryman's ironic comment on the marked increase in Supreme Court activity since Roosevelt's inauguration—an allusion to the president's seemingly endless plans for reforming the country.

constituted a violation of the contract clause in the federal Constitution and of the due process and equal protection clauses of the Fourteenth Amendment. Against this was placed the argument of emergency need. The court sustained the Minnesota Act, ruling that in this case, emergency furnished occasion for the exercise of power. It also stressed that the act was temporary.

THE "GOLD CLAUSE" CASES

The "Gold Clause" required the payment in gold of interest as well as capital on existing government and private contracts. A joint resolution of June 5, 1933, abro-gated the gold clause so that nearly all kinds of money became legal tender for the payment of mortgages. The legislation brought about four legal suits, two against the government and two against railroad companies. One plaintiff held liberty bonds, one

The Four Needs

President Roosevelt outlined four needs to be satisfied if the U.S. Supreme Court was to function effectively, including new personnel and a greater emphasis on speed and efficiency in dealing with constitutional matters.

"First, to eliminate congestion of calendars and to make the judiciary as a whole less static by the constant and systematic addition of new blood to its personnel; second, to make the judiciary more elastic by providing for temporary transfers of circuit and district judges to those places where federal courts are most in arrears; third, to furnish the Supreme Court practical assistance in supervising the conduct of business in the lower courts; fourth, to eliminate inequality, uncertainty, and delay now existing in the determination of constitutional questions involving federal statutes.

"If we increase the personnel of the federal courts so that cases may be promptly decided…and may be given adequate and prompt hearing on all appeals; if we invigorate all the courts by the persistent infusion of new blood; if we grant to the Supreme Court further power and responsibility in maintaining the efficiency of the entire federal judiciary; and if we assure government participation in the speedier consideration and final determination of all constitutional questions, we shall go a long way toward our high objectives. If these measures achieve their aim, we may be relieved of the necessity of considering any fundamental changes in the powers of the courts or the constitution of our government—changes which involve consequences so far-reaching as to cause uncertainty as to the wisdom of such course."

gold certificates, and two railroad obligations. All the securities in question bore the gold clause. The plaintiffs claimed that the abrogation defrauded them of property due to them under the gold clause. On February 18, 1935, the Supreme Court made

Supreme Court Justices

The following Supreme Court justices served during Roosevelt's presidency. Their terms of service appear after their names.

Willis Van Devanter
  (1911–1937)
James C. McReynolds
  (1914–1941)
Louis D. Brandeis
  (1916–1939)
George Sutherland
  (1922–1938)
Pierce Butler (1922–1939)
Harlan F. Stone (1925–1946;
  Chief Justice 1941–1946)
Charles Evans Hughes
  (1930–1941; Chief Justice
  1930–1941)
Owen J. Roberts
  (1930–1945)
Benjamin N. Cardozo
  (1932–1938)
Hugo L. Black (1937–1971)
Stanley Reed (1938–1957)
Felix Frankfurter
  (1939–1962)
William O. Douglas
  (1939–1975)
Frank Murphy (1940–1949)
James F. Byrnes (1941–1942)
Robert H. Jackson
  (1941–1954)
Wiley B. Rutledge
  (1943–1949)

its decision on the cases. In the two private railroad contracts the decision was 5–4 against the plaintiffs and in support of the abrogation. The Court argued that private contracts had no power to interfere with the rights given by the Constitution to Congress to "coin money and regulate the value thereof." With regard to the gold certificates the Court also decided against the plaintiff, since, had he received his payment in gold dollars, he would have had to turn them over to the government in exchange for other forms of currency under constitutional law. In the case of the liberty bonds, however, the Court declared the actions of the government to be unconstitutional. It ruled the government's refusal to pay its own obligations in gold a breach of faith. Overall, however, the government had almost managed a clear victory.

LEGISLATION AND LITIGATION

By 1934 over a thousand cases involving New Deal legislation were in litigation. Many of them reached the Supreme Court,

where individual judges, most of whom were conservative Republicans, could issue injunctions against laws passed by Congress. The situation created serious problems for the New Deal.

By 1935 the Supreme Court had declared the NRA outside the boundaries set by the Constitution. Only a fragment of the legislation survived the Supreme Court, becoming the core of the NLRA, which to this day is honored by workers of the nation as their "bill of rights."

Congress continued to pass laws to support Roosevelt's plan to overturn the country's economic situation. It authorized the creation of the Works Progress Administration and the National Labor Relations Board, and passed several measures to support workers, facilitate employment, and aid economic recovery. They included the Banking Act of 1935, the Emergency Relief Appropriation Act, and the Social Security Act.

The economy was recovering: By the end of 1935 unemployment had fallen to 20.1 percent; and the gross national product, the value of the goods and services produced in a year, had grown 8.1 percent. The battle between the judiciary and the New Deal continued, however. In 1935 and 1936 the U.S. Supreme Court had struck down eight of Roosevelt's New Deal programs.

Justice Benjamin N. Cardozo (1870–1938) was a liberal who influenced judicial decisions in the direction of greater involvement with public policy and the updating of legal principles. He was appointed to the Supreme Court by President Hoover following the resignation of Justice Oliver Wendell Holmes, Jr., in January 1932.

3. ROOSEVELT'S ATTEMPTS TO REFORM THE SUPREME COURT

Public sentiment against the judiciary intensified, and many critics questioned whether judicial review was itself constitutional. As a result several constitutional amendments were introduced into Congress in 1936. One would require a two-thirds vote of the Court whenever an act of Congress was declared unconstitutional, while another would permit Congress to revalidate federal laws previously declared unconstitutional by passing them with a two-thirds vote in both houses. A third proposal would abolish altogether the Court's power to declare the federal laws unconstitutional. None of the proposed amendments ever reached legislative status.

Amid all the changes Roosevelt originally remained silent, hoping that the weight of public sentiment would force the Court to remove the obstacles it was putting in his way without him having to enter the battle. In his election campaign of 1936, for example, he made no reference to the Court's position (see Volume 2, Chapter 6, "The Election of 1936"). In 1937, however, the Supreme Court challenged yet another New Deal body: the NLRB was deemed to be in contravention of the Constitution. After his election victory Roosevelt submitted a plan for "judicial reform" that has come to be known as his attempt to "pack" the Supreme Court.

A NEW STRATEGY

Realizing that the sentiment of the people was not about to change the attitudes of the Supreme Court, Roosevelt decided to try a different strategy. He felt it essential to reform the Supreme Court because their decisions made it impossible for him to implement the changes he felt the country needed to pull itself out of the Great Depression. He felt increasingly that the government was stripped of its power to deal effectively with the nation's economic problems. On February 5, 1937, he submitted to Congress a plan for judicial reform.

THE COURT-PACKING PLAN

Roosevelt and his attorney general, Homer Cummings (1870–1956), considered several options. They might have attacked the issue of judicial review head-on, as the amendments proposed by Congress would have done. This ran the danger of offending a public that saw the judiciary as the protector of the Constitution. Instead, therefore, they attempted to change the number of justices on the Court to alter its political makeup. This was not a new idea. It had been done six times since 1789. The new plan did have a twist to it, though, because it proposed adding a new justice for every justice over the age of 70 who refused to retire.

The plan had extra appeal because Justice Department

Justice Louis D. Brandeis (1856–1941) was the first Jew to sit on the Supreme Court. As a liberal, he supported most of the New Deal reforms, although he opposed both the NIRA and the AAA as unconstitutional. He was a defender of people's rights and hated "bigness" in government and business.

lawyers had discovered that Justice James C. McReynolds, one of the most conservative justices then sitting on the Court, had proposed the same idea in 1913, while acting as attorney general in the government of President Woodrow Wilson. Roosevelt went ahead with the plan without consulting Congress. Critics insisted that the president's proposal masked his true intention, which was to fill the judiciary with his own men. As it happened, his efforts succeeded only in alienating a number of conservative Democrats and caused a party split that would never fully heal.

CONVINCING CONGRESS

In a February address Roosevelt bemoaned the heavy strain under which the U.S. Supreme Court was operating. The burden of materials and evidence to be analyzed was becoming, he said, too much for the judiciary. In many cases hearings were turned down and appeals refused. Out of 867 petitions for review by the Supreme Court only 150 had actually been heard. He therefore questioned the justification of a judiciary that had to turn down 87 percent of the cases presented to it by private litigants.

Further, the judiciary had thrown out many of the acts passed by Congress—this Roosevelt felt was untenable. The justices were taking on a role that was not given to them by the Constitution. By questioning and debating the validity of an act that had been deemed constitutional by the legislative and executive branches

Cartoonist Clifford Berryman's mocking analogy between Harold Ickes' unnecessary PWA building schemes and Roosevelt's plan to enlarge the Supreme Court.

of government, he argued, the judiciary was increasingly taking on the additional function of a third house of the national legislature.

Roosevelt fell back on a law passed in 1919, which provided that the president could, on finding a judge over 70 years of age "unable to discharge efficiently all the duties of his office by reason of

•

"…unable to discharge efficiently all the duties of his office."

•

mental or physical disability of permanent character," appoint additional district and circuit judges. Roosevelt, however, sought to appoint new judges on the basis of a choice made by the aged

judges themselves. If they retired at age 70, no additional justice would be added to the Court; but if they decided to stay in office, an additional judge would be added to compensate, enlarging the Supreme Court to a maximum of 15 justices.

Basing his position on the precedent set by the attorney general earlier in the century, Roosevelt made the following proposal to Congress: "I have recently called the attention of the Congress to the dire need for a comprehensive program to reorganize the administrative machinery of the executive branch of our government. I now make a similar recommendation to the Congress in regard to the judicial branch of the government, in order that it also may function in accord with modern necessities."

The meat of his argument lay with the supposed old age of the judges. He implied that they

adequate job. Still, he called for a means of supplementing the Court with new blood so that the work of the justices could be carried out with the full vigor it demanded.

REACTION

Reaction to Roosevelt's proposal was intense. It was expected that the Republicans would be the first to denounce the proposals, but the chairman of the House Judiciary Committee, Democrat Hatton Sumners, acted to effectively kill the program before it had gotten off the ground. A further argument against implementing the plan came in another, unexpected form. The Court began to reverse its earlier conservative course by ruling in favor of legislation that it might previously have denounced. The justices carried out what was dubbed "the switch in time that saved nine." They began voting in favor of legislation passed by Congress.

4. CHANGE OF OUTLOOK AT COURT

In March 1937 Justice Owen J. Roberts, who had been a staunch adherent of conservative ideology, suddenly adopted a markedly liberal allegiance. This tilted the balance in the Court from a majority against New Deal legislation to a 5–4 majority in its favor. In a pivotal case Justice Roberts chose to uphold a minimum wage law in Washington State; the ruling was in direct opposition to the Lochner case verdict in New York State. Two weeks later another shift took place. The NLRA guaranteed the right of workers to form unions in interstate commerce businesses; dismissal or discrimination by employers because of such union membership and its activities would be punished. In *National*

Sculptor Edgardo Simone completes a bust of Supreme Court Justice Harlan Fiske Stone in 1930. Like liberal justices Cardozo and Brandeis, Stone voted to uphold the unemployment insurance and old-age provision aspects of the Social Security Act. He was bitterly opposed to the Tipaldo case verdict, in which a judicial majority ruled that a New York State minimum wage law was an unconstitutional infringement on freedom of contract.

maintained their posts beyond their ability to carry out their duties because they had no viable alternative in the form of adequate pension provision. Of these justices he said "When after 80 years of our national history the Congress made provision for pensions, it found a well-entrenched tradition among judges to cling to their posts, in many instances far beyond their years of physical or mental capacity. Their salaries were small. As with other men, responsibilities and obligations accumulated. No alternative had been open to them except to attempt to perform the duties of their offices to the very edge of the

grave." The oldest judge at the time, Louis Brandeis, was 80. Ironically, he was one of the most liberal judges sitting on the court.

Roosevelt went on to describe the complexity of the judicial system and the need for younger, more agile brains to cope with the strain. It was no longer a question

•

"…a well-entrenched tradition among judges to cling to their posts…"

•

of merely sitting down and arguing a point. "Records and briefs must be read," he stated, "statutes, decisions, and extensive material of a technical, scientific, statistical and economic nature must be searched and studied; opinions must be formulated and written. The modern tasks of judges call for the use of full energies." He did admit that there were some judges of advanced age who could do an

Labor Relations Board v. Jones & Laughlin Steel Corp., 1937, the Supreme Court upheld the act by a slim majority of 5–4. It ruled that the legislation fell within the parameters of the Constitution and was a legitimate exercise of executive authority. This was a clear signal that the Court would no longer interfere with the executive in its attempts at regulating the economy.

The turnaround by the Court seemed to remove the need for FDR's bill. Congressmen, feeling more justified in opposing it, urged him to withdraw it. The president, however, was confident of his success in Congress and, eager to guarantee a majority vote for proposals that were part of the

"Yes, you gave me authority to pick my kind of umpire last November!" This 1937 cartoon shows Roosevelt reminding his critics that his 1936 election victory indicated public support for his reforms.

New Deal, pushed for the bill to be passed. Letters and radio broadcasts showed people rallying both for and against Roosevelt.

LOSS OF FACE

Roosevelt's refusal to back down increased the pressure and tension within Congress. The Republican opposition naturally came out as a violent opponent of the bill. What was more worrying for the administration was the reaction within Roosevelt's Democratic Party. A majority of Roosevelt's own side was turning against him. They felt that they had been cheated: Roosevelt had not announced his proposal before Congress nor put it through the customary channels before it was presented to the legislature. The secrecy with which he had acted lost him credibility and attracted criticism from Republicans and liberals alike.

The Judiciary Committees of both houses were now set to review

Opposition to Packing the Court

A letter by Frank E. Gannett, publisher of Gannett Newspapers, Rochester, N.Y., and one of the most outspoken members of the press, argued against "packing" the Supreme Court. The letter was sent to the Office of the Solicitor in the Justice Department and then referred to the attorney general. Like other letters in the department file, it expresses concern that the real issue is the expansion of executive powers. He wrote: "President Roosevelt has cleverly camouflaged a most amazing and startling proposal for packing the Supreme Court. It is true that the lower courts are slow and overburdened, we probably do need more judges to expedite litigation, but this condition should not be used as a subtle excuse for changing the complexion and undermining the independence of our highest court. Increasing the number of judges from nine to fifteen would not make this high tribunal act any more promptly than it does now, but it would give the president control of the Judiciary Department." Gannett believed, as did many, that Roosevelt's real goal was to gain control of the court, not to improve its efficiency.

THE SUPREME COURT • 39

the bill. Roosevelt won by a majority of 100 in the House; however, Hatton Sumners of Texas, chair of the House Judiciary Committee, declaring his displeasure at the whole event, refused to hold hearings on the bill. Although the president considered taking votes to compel the Judiciary Committee to report on the bill, he abandoned the cause and began hearings on the bill in the Senate instead.

PLEA TO THE PEOPLE

Hoping to win the support and trust of the people in this matter, Roosevelt delivered one of the most significant of his fireside chats to the nation on March 9, 1937. "Last Thursday I described the American form of government as a three-horse team provided by the Constitution to the American people so that their field might be plowed. The three horses are, of course, the three branches of government— the Congress, the Executive, and the Courts. Two of the horses are pulling in unison today; the third is not. Those who have intimated that the president of the United States is trying to drive that team overlook the simple fact

The Supreme Court is under attack from all sides in this ironic comment.

Support for Reform

Robert M. La Follette, Jr., a Wisconsin senator, summed up the arguments of Roosevelt's supporters in an NBC radio broadcast on February 13, 1937:

"The Founding Fathers were firm believers in a system of checks and of balances: They believed in the separation of powers, but there is no evidence that they believed in the uncontrolled supremacy of any one of the three great branches of government over the other two. 'It must be remembered,' Mr. Justice Holmes said, 'that the legislatures are ultimate guardians of the liberties and welfare of the people in quite as great degree as the courts.'

"Article I of the Constitution specifically provides that 'all legislative powers herein granted shall be vested in the Congress of the United States.' The Founding Fathers never dreamed that legislative policies adopted by the Congress in carrying out powers clearly delegated to it were to be subject to a rigid judicial review amounting to a judicial veto. Proposals to give the Supreme Court even a limited veto power over legislation were rejected by an overwhelming vote in the Constitutional Convention....

"The idea of an unchecked supremacy of the Supreme Court has been built up only over the last forty years. It has been built up by corporation lawyers of the Liberty League ilk who have tried in the Court to counteract the reforms, like popular election of senators, which are designed to make the will of the people the law of the land. It has been indoctrinated in our schools and in our thinking with the same conscious direction as the propaganda of the public utilities. If the Congress continues to acquiesce in such a pernicious doctrine, the Congress will be guilty of abandoning its constitutional rights and duties. The Constitution provides for a separation of powers, not for a judicial supremacy. The idea of judicial supremacy is not found in the Constitution or the writings of the Constitutional Fathers. It is an idea of smart lawyers who, beaten in the Congress, have sought for their own advantage to twist and distort the Constitution ever since its adoption."

that the president, as chief executive, is himself one of the three horses."

Roosevelt then began a defense against the allegations of court packing. He went on to explain what exactly he had been charged with—that he "wished to place on the bench spineless puppets who would disregard the law and would decide specific cases as I wished them to be decided." Roosevelt went on to argue that he wished to appoint justices who understood the modern conditions, who would not override the judgment of the Congress on legislative policy, and who would act as justices and not as legislators. The president described his detractors as people who fundamentally objected to modern social and economic legislation and those who believed that the amendment process is best but could not as yet agree on one. He went on to express his belief that the people of America were in

Opposition to the Bill

Democrats Carter Glass, Harry Byrd, Millard Tydings, and Burton K. Wheeler began a campaign directly opposing the president's court reform bill and his administrative tactics. Wheeler, a liberal, had a reputation for honest, courageous leadership and was a natural choice to front the cause. Although a critic of the Court, he was an adamant believer in the Constitution and the system of government as set up by the Founders. He saw Roosevelt's plan as interfering with the independence of the judiciary and became the spokesman of Democratic opposition to the bill, a move that was deemed political suicide. The Democratic Party's unity was seriously damaged by the split.

agreement with him and that they should not be fooled by the arguments of people who acted against the best interests of the American worker.

Although it was a powerful speech, the broadcast did not have the impact Roosevelt had hoped for. Burton K. Wheeler, leader of

the campaign opposing the bill, stepped up his attack and called on well-known liberals to speak before the House Committee. This was a profoundly astute maneuver, since all the chosen speakers were considered to be of great integrity and, as liberals, could not be questioned on their loyalty to their country, the Constitution, or the cause of social reform. There followed lawyers, teachers, Constitutional authorities, civil servants, writers, leaders of the opposition, and other factions. All rejected entirely the notion that the judiciary should be reorganized, despite its interference with FDR's New Deal legislation.

VAN DEVANTER RESIGNS
To further complicate matters, Justice Willis Van Devanter (1859–1941), one of the oldest and most conservative justices, resigned from the Court, giving Roosevelt the opportunity to fill

After his retirement in 1937 Justice Willis Van Devanter ponders Roosevelt's delay in replacing him after the president had spent so long trying to create new justices.

Supreme Court justices in their robes on November 1, 1991. President Bill Clinton's nomination of Associate Justice Clarence Thomas (left of picture), who had been involved in a harassment case, provides a more recent example of a controversial appointment to the court by the U.S. president.

and withdrew from the conflict, leaving Garner to deal with the details. The court bill was dead, and with it FDR's battle with the Supreme Court. He appointed a further seven judges during his presidency and in 1941, when Charles Evans Hughes retired, he promoted the liberal Republican Harlan Stone to chief justice. The court endorsed federal regulation of the economy in World War II.

A satirical comment on Roosevelt's nomination of William O. Douglas (aged 41) to the court in 1939, upon the retirement of Justice Brandeis at age 83.

YOUR HONORS, HE'S YOUNG, BUT HE'S TOUGH! WATCH HIM.

U.S. SUPREME COURT

the vacancy with someone close to his own political leaning. The Senate, however, wanted to appoint Senator Joe Robinson—he was largely responsible for the survival of the New Deal and Roosevelt's associated plans, and they felt he should be rewarded for his loyalty. But the president, feeling that Robinson was too much of a reactionary to gain support from the liberals of his party, decided to appoint a liberal senator. To many of his colleagues this was the final straw. They protested angrily, and Robinson's coolness toward the Roosevelt administration forced the president to offer him the appointment after all. It was not taken up, however, as Robinson

died suddenly of a heart attack. Eventually Roosevelt appointed Hugo Black as the ninth justice.

DEATH OF THE BILL

By this time matters in the Senate chambers were heated and deteriorating rapidly. Vice President John N. Garner had departed for his home state of Texas, leaving Roosevelt to deal with the situation on his own. After Robinson's funeral Garner declared that the time had come for a settlement. Roosevelt agreed

3

HUEY LONG

Huey Long (1893–1935), known as the "King-fish," was one of the Depression era's most controversial figures. To many working-class Americans, particularly in his native Louisiana, the folksy, charismatic politician was a hero fighting for the common man. To many others he was a corrupt authoritarian well described as "the most colorful, as well as the most dangerous, man…in American politics."

Faced with the dire economic conditions of the 1930s, when workers could not find work and farming families were losing their farms, people were eager to hear promises of a brighter future. Left- and right-leaning populist political movements calling for reform of society gained massive support. Charismatic leaders such as Dr. Francis Townsend and Father Charles Coughlin became prominent national figures (see Volume 4,

A statue of Huey Long still stands outside the state capitol he had built in Baton Rouge, Louisiana.

Sharing the Wealth

Long's radical proposal to redistribute wealth from rich to poor Americans is summed up in a speech he made as U.S. senator, from which this extract comes:

"How many men ever went to a barbecue and would let one man take off the table what's intended for nine-tenths of the people to eat? The only way you'll ever be able to feed the balance of the people is to make that man come back and bring back some of that grub he ain't got no business with.

"Now, how you gonna feed the balance of the people? What's [magnates] Morgan and Baruch and Rockefeller and Mellon gonna do with all that grub? They can't eat it. They can't wear the clothes. They can't live in the house.

"But when they've got everything on God's living Earth that they can eat and they can wear and they can live in, and all that their children can live in and wear and eat, and all their children's children can use, then we got

to call Mr. Morgan and Mr. Mellon and Mr. Rockefeller back and say... 'Put that stuff back on this table here that you took away from here that you don't need. Leave something else for the American people to consume.'"

Long cuts a dashing figure in a white suit as he steps from a train in this 1930s image. As ever, he is ready to greet the waiting public.

Chapter 4, "The Right-wing Backlash," and Volume 5, Chapter 3, "Society in the 1930s"). From his power base in Louisiana the most influential of the populists, Huey Long, won millions of admirers with his calls for the redistribution of wealth from rich to poor.

AIMS AND IDEALS

Long claimed to support the "little man" in the face of powerful business interests. He proclaimed the injustice of a situation in which "four percent of the American people own 85 percent of the wealth of America and that over 70 percent of the people of America don't own enough to pay the debts that they owe." Long's campaign came at a time when President Franklin D. Roosevelt (1882–1945) was already attempting to improve the nation's economy with his New Deal.

Long considered Roosevelt too middle-of-the road, however, and too readily influenced by bankers, Wall Street, and big business. Long's proposal to guarantee every U.S. citizen a minimum annual income had a wide

Long's easy charm, apparent in this early photograph, was coupled with a ruthless streak that enabled him to brush aside opposition.

national appeal. By 1935 eight million people belonged to his Share-Our-Wealth Society (see box, page 52), and an average of 20,000 new members were joining daily. In 1935 an assassin's bullet ended Huey Long's challenge for the presidency. But the Louisiana political machine that he created lasted many years after his death.

1. EARLY YEARS

Huey Pierce Long was born on August 30, 1893, near Winnfield, Winn Parish, Louisiana. He was the eighth of nine children in a middle-class Baptist farming family. In his early years Long was much influenced by the political ideas that flourished in Winn Parish. During the 1890s the Populist movement, which fought

Threshing rice in 1930s Louisiana. Farmers made up a large part of Long's constituency. He won their support by promising a better life.

for farmers' rights, was influential there. Later, in the years leading up to World War I (1914–1918) the area also had strong socialist sympathies.

EDUCATION

Little is known about Long's childhood, although his domineering nature was clearly marked by the time he reached high school. There were regular confrontations with the school

•

"…the most colorful, as well as the most dangerous, man…in American politics."

•

authorities, and in his senior year Long printed handbills critical of the teachers. As a result he was thrown out and had to find a job.

Over the next four years Long was employed variously as a door-to-door salesman, an auctioneer, a book peddler, and a vegetable oil

pitchman. Then, however, he gave up work to study law. After a brief period at Oklahoma University he returned to Louisiana to enroll at Tulane University, New Orleans.

Despite studying at all these institutions, Long never earned a high school or college diploma. This was no reflection on his ability as a student. Long was largely self-taught: He read every law book he could find. At the age of just 22 he passed a special bar examination. Long had completed just a year of study. Most people took the examination after three.

POLITICAL LIFE

In 1915 Long started work as a lawyer in Winnfield. Then, after moving to Shreveport, Louisiana, and practicing there, he broke into politics. By that time Long was married and had told his wife, Rose, that he planned to become both governor of Louisiana and president of the United States.

Huey Long's election to the Louisiana Railroad Commission, on which he served from 1918 to 1928, was his first step in that direction. In 1921 the Railroad Commission became the much more influential Public Service

Long appealed to poor Louisiana fishermen as well as farmers. In the Depression many struggled to survive in their simple wooden homes on the Mississippi bayous.

Commission, and Long's power grew. Borrowing the name of a character from the popular *Amos 'n' Andy* radio program, Long started referring to himself as "Kingfish." The name stuck throughout his political career, even after he believed it had outlived its usefulness. In 1924 Long was reelected to the commission and became its chairman. By then he was also the state's attorney for public utility litigation. But he wanted more.

GOING FOR GOVERNOR

In 1924 Huey Long set his sights firmly on the Louisiana governor's mansion, but he was narrowly defeated for the Democratic nomination. In 1928, the same year he became a Democratic national committeeman, Long announced his second candidacy for the nomination. He outlined what he saw as the state's needs: "This state shows every need for a constructive administration, devoted to the protection and expansion of labor and capital, industry, and agriculture, all working toward the efficiency of our courts, public schools, freedom in religious beliefs, and reduction in taxation and burdens of government, and toward liberating our state and our institutions from the ever growing modern tendency of monopoly and concentration of power."

LOUISIANA LIFE

In the late 1920s Louisiana was populated mainly by poor and uneducated farmers. The highway system was a collection of muddy lanes—there were only 300 miles of paved roads. The state had only

Louisiana Past

Huey Long's home state had a complex history that contributed to the distinctive nature of its people and politics. The original French colony of Louisiana, founded in the 17th century, covered a larger area on both sides of the Mississippi. The region was divided between the British and the Spanish in the 18th century, then briefly returned to French control before being purchased by the U.S. government in 1803. The state of Louisiana entered the Union in 1812.

From the 18th century onward many major plantations growing cotton, sugar, and other crops were established all across the state. Black slaves provided the labor needed to run them.

Partly in defense of the right to own slaves, Louisiana seceded from the Union in 1861. Then, in the Civil War (1861–1865) it fought with the Confederacy against Union forces. In 1865 the U.S. government made slavery illegal. In 1868, three years after the Union victory, Louisiana adopted a constitution that gave black people voting rights. But unrest between blacks and whites continued.

When Huey Long was elected governor in 1928, he inherited a state whose economy was still dominated by agriculture, and where there was still tension between blacks and whites. He skillfully appealed to the concerns and prejudices of poor farmers. But he always refused to play the race card.

Louisianans protest in New Orleans in 1930 about numerous causes, including Long's failure to provide food for the unemployed.

three major bridges, and they had high toll charges. The ferries were antique. Of America's 48 states, Louisiana ranked next-to-last in literacy and 39th in average gross, or pretax, income.

Louisiana's wealthy political establishment—men with their power base in the city of New Orleans and on huge plantations—controlled the state. The so-called cotton kings, rice kings, sugar kings, lumber kings, and other major plantation-owners kept their workers in debt and crushed efforts to organize labor. According to one Long associate, "Ten thousand aristocrats ruled the state, while two million common people wallowed in slavery."

Huey Long found his strength in attacking Louisiana's powerful men, the "Old Regulars," and appealing to its downtrodden masses. The rural poor were very

receptive to his promises of public works programs and free textbooks for every schoolchild. Long's egalitarian campaign slogan, "Every Man a King, But No Man Wears a Crown," helped him triumph over the New Orleans Democratic machine, win the nomination, then sweep boldly into the governor's mansion.

2. GOVERNOR LONG
On May 21, 1928, Huey Long took office and set out to become the strongest governor Louisiana had known. In other parts of the country his program would have been thought reasonably conventional for a progressive politician. In archly conservative Louisiana his arrival brought revolution to the political and social landscape. The new governor snubbed Louisiana's elite and refused to entertain

The impressive, 34-story state capitol in Baton Rouge, Louisiana, was built on the orders of Huey Long and completed in 1932.

socially or to attend grand banquets. The grand governor's mansion, where the feet of the privileged had once trod, now welcomed the muddy shoes of Long's associates. Breaking firmly away from both Republican conservatives and Democrats, Long offered a clearly defined alternative to the old two-party system. Although officially a Democrat, he lost the support of many party members through his self-aggrandizing behavior.

LONG'S POLITICAL MACHINE
Long began to strengthen the executive by creating a powerful political machine through which he could control the various, traditionally separate, institutions of state government. Most of the state Supreme Court members were under Long's influence. His State Printing Board had great economic power, and was almost able to silence the rural and smalltown press of Louisiana.

Having risen to power as a result of the public's discontent with years of corrupt and short-

sighted rule by conservatives, Long was quickly able to win a large and enthusiastic following for his policies. Despite his vast support base among poor whites, he was the first major Southern politician not to resort to race-based politics. Instead, he appealed to the working class as a whole and fought for much greater political participation by both poor blacks and whites through the elimination of the poll tax.

REFORM PROGRAMS

True to his promise, Long gave every community free textbooks for its schoolchildren. Setting out on his program of economic and social reform, the new governor revised tax codes to place heavier payments on corporations, particularly oil companies. Natural resources like oil, gas, and lumber were hit with severance taxes. Gas, telephone, and electricity rates were cut. The wealthy were hit by an inheritance tax.

Louisiana's weak infrastructure and social services were transformed. The state-owned Charity

A Harsh Assessment

Opposition to Huey Long among Louisiana's conservative "Old Regulars" and their families was fierce. Many did not hesitate to express their views freely in the media. During an interview with Shreveport radio, Anne Pleasant, the wife of former Louisiana governor Riffun Pleasant, described Long in these harsh terms: "[He] has not only common ways, but a common, sordid, dirty soul [with] the greed and coarseness of the swine…the venom of the snake, and the cruel cowardice of the skulking hyena." Long remained completely undeterred by such outspoken taunts.

Hospital System was set up, bridges built, and nearly 13,000 miles of roads paved. The public school system was extended into rural areas, and night schools ran vigorous adult literacy programs. Louisiana State University gained a medical school. Long brought natural gas to New Orleans and increased funding for its port.

SUPPORT AND OPPOSITION

Among Louisiana's rural poor Long achieved almost godlike status: It was not uncommon to

see the governor's photo hanging on the walls of backwoods shacks. However, Long also had many fierce opponents. Louisiana's conservatives hated him. They despised his attacks on the old economic and political power structure and believed that his grandiose development plans were financially unsound. The new governor's emotional public speeches and power to stir up the masses also unnerved them.

Nationally, Long came to be known as the dictator of Louisiana.

Long surveys his mail in 1932. His outspoken views always brought him large amounts of mail from admirers and opponents alike.

While promising to make every man a king, he and only he wore the crown of authority. Long tore down the old governor's mansion in the state capital of Baton Rouge and erected a new one. He also constructed a new bronze-and-marble state capitol building in the city. Such extravagance at a time when many people were suffering abject poverty was much criticized.

POWER AND PATRONAGE

As Louisiana governor Huey Long established a wide-ranging system of patronage, appointing his unconditional supporters to powerful government positions. Opponents in the state legislature were either forced or bribed into passing the laws that he wanted.

By the time Long abandoned his gubernatorial duties, he was in firm control of Louisiana's power structure—everything from local municipalities to the state's bureaucracy and courts of law. As Hodding Carter, publisher of the *Hammond Courier* newspaper, put it: "No public officeholder, no teacher, no fire chief or fireman, no police chief or policeman, no day laborer on state projects held his job [without consent from the

Long machine].... Long could have taxed to extinction any business...and business knew it. Men could be—and were—arrested by unidentified men, the members of [Long's] secret police, held incommunicado, tried, and found guilty on trumped-up charges."

IMPEACHMENT AND ESCAPE

Prompted by conservatives, the Louisiana legislature impeached Long in 1929 on charges of bribery, misuse of state funds, and unauthorized destruction of the governor's mansion, as well as "incompetency, corruption...and gross misconduct." The claimed misconduct included cursing and attempting to hire an assassin. The main impetus behind the impeachment may have been resentment over Long's successful push to introduce a constitutional amendment allowing the taxation of state oil interests.

Staring political oblivion in the face, Long managed to convince sufficient senators—they were afterwards known as the "Famous Fifteen"—to sign an agreement that they would not vote to convict him. But the near-miss hardened the governor and drove him to create a power structure that his enemies could not easily attack.

3. SENATOR LONG

In 1931 Long's opponents in the state legislature defeated his plans for a major expansion of the state highway program. He did not back down but stated instead that he would take the issue directly to the people as a candidate for the U.S. Senate. In the event that he were elected, Long said, he might not occupy the Senate seat right

A photograph of Huey Long's 1929 impeachment trial on display in Louisiana's Old State Capitol. It is part of a state history exhibition.

> ## "I ain't no fish! I'm gonna pick another name, maybe one with a lion…in it."

away, but stay on as Louisiana governor until the highway construction was in progress.

Although he was only halfway through his term as governor, the "Kingfish" was elected to the U.S. Senate in 1930. He boldly proclaimed, "I ain't no fish! I'm gonna pick another name, maybe one with a lion or a tiger in it." His term as senator began on March 4, 1931, but Long refused to take up his new office until he had found a stalwart supporter to replace him as governor.

THE STRUGGLE FOR SUCCESSION

Finding a loyal replacement was not an easy task. Long fell out with his lieutenant governor, Paul Cyr, and was not prepared to leave the governorship in his hands. Cyr, however, had his own ideas. He argued strongly that the governor had abandoned his office the moment he was elected U.S. senator. Then, in a half-baked coup attempt in October 1931, Cyr found a justice of the peace and took the oath as governor.

True to his trademark theatricality, Long summoned the highway police, the state police, and the Louisiana National Guard.

In this 1932 photograph Huey Long prepares for his swearing-in ceremony as U.S. senator. With him is his wife, Rose McConnell Long.

The governor's office and mansion were surrounded by motorized troops, supposedly to keep Cyr from seizing power. The move was largely symbolic. But Long's next step, to use Cyr's own reasoning against him, was in earnest.

Since the lieutenant governor had become governor, Long now argued, it followed that he had vacated the lieutenant governor's post. In accordance with Louisiana law, the Senate president had to fill that position. Senate president Alvin O. King was one of Long's supporters. Once King had taken the oath as lieutenant governor, Cyr was out of a job.

Before leaving for Washington, Long wielded his power to get one

of his own men elected into the governor's mansion. O. K. "Oscar" Allen was considered the weakest of the Kingfish's aides, making him the ideal replacement for a man planning to rule from afar. Even after Allen was elected governor, Long kept him firmly in his place.

LONG IN WASHINGTON

Huey Long finally resigned as state governor on January 25, 1932, leaving behind a powerful political machine ready to carry out his specific orders and programs. With Louisiana now his undisputed turf, Long set his sights on the nation's capital.

Long's January 1932 arrival at the U.S. Senate in Washington,

Press Censorship

Long kept the Louisiana press firmly under his own control. One example of his censorship tactics came in 1934. In that year Long rival and state senator J. Y. Sanders, Jr., was elected to the U.S. House of Representatives. Sanders had once staged an assembly of supporters to get himself elected locally, so in order to ridicule him Long set up a mock assembly that voted LSU football star Abe Mickal into the office of state senator. An LSU student wrote a letter to the student newspaper *Daily Reveille* asking, "Is there one serious-minded student in the University…

in sympathy with the proposed attempt to seat a popular member of the LSU football squad in the La. Senate? What a mockery of constitutional government and democracy to elect by mass meeting a member of La.'s governing body."

Long saw the letter as the paper was going to print and reportedly yelled, "That's my university, and I'm not going to stand for any criticism from anybody out there." Under pressure from Long, LSU president Jim Smith stopped the presses, telling the editor that "[I] would rather fire [you], [your] staff, destroy the School of Journalism, and fire 4,000 students before [I] would offend the Senator." Students fought back with a petition that made national news. The Long machine used strong-arm tactics to get an apology and retraction from the students, though seven refused to back down. These "Reveille Seven" were soon expelled.

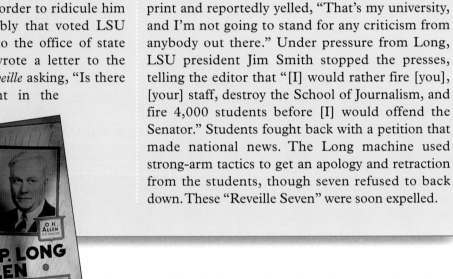

This poster promoting Long and Allen, his successor as Louisiana governor, is also in the Old State Capitol exhibition.

D.C., was anything but discreet. His brash demeanor and disrespect for protocol brought instant political enemies on both sides of the aisle.

Senate tradition held that new senators be escorted down the aisle to take their oath. The man to accompany Long should have been fellow Louisiana senator Edwin Broussard, but the two men were on bad terms. Long had helped Broussard, a south Louisiana Roman Catholic, get elected against the odds by securing him the support of voters in the north Louisiana Bible Belt. When Long had then announced his intention to run for the Senate, however, Broussard had come out in support of the incumbent, Joseph Ransdell. For this reason Long broke with tradition on his very first day in the Senate,

choosing to be escorted not by Broussard but instead by the Democratic leader, Joe Robinson.

Senators were variously amused or appalled as the Kingfish carried his lighted cigar down the aisle and left it on the leader's desk to take his oath. Afterward the freshman senator wandered casually around the chamber, throwing his arms over the shoulders of senators or slapping them heartily on the back.

Breaking the rules from the start, Long quickly and deliberately set out to draw his new colleagues' attention to his rural ways. An extroverted, master orator with the ability to debate both domestic and foreign issues skillfully, Long spoke fast and in the Southern vernacular. His wit and sarcasm often caused the other senators to burst out in laughter, but also created enemies.

LONG AND ROBINSON

Long was a particular nuisance to Joe Robinson (1872–1937), the Democratic leader. A dominating personality in his own right, Robinson clashed often with the flamboyant senator. Long once read the corporate client list of Robinson's Arkansas law firm into the Congressional Record. Then, with mock sincerity, he asked if there might be potential conflicts between Robinson's political and professional interests. One Senate observer would later recall, "I can see Joe Robinson now going all the way down that empty row to Long, talking at the top of his voice and putting his fist under Long's face as he stood over him. Robinson was shaking his fist under Long's chin, roaring out his words. Long, seated, looked meanwhile at the ceiling as if he heard nothing...." The incident turned Robinson into one of Long's permanent enemies.

SPEAKING STYLE

Long's oratory was highly effective. He was especially fond of spouting dubious quotes from the Bible and from the works of William Shakespeare. The Senate chamber's walls at that time had decorative recesses, and in the recess near his desk Long kept a Shakespearean concordance and a Bible concordance. In the midst of debate he would grab one of the volumes to fish for just the right passage. So frequently did Long turn to biblical quotes that he gave a copy of the Bible to the Senate debate reporters for reference. They used the same volume for several decades.

Long gives a speech in Chicago in 1932. He put body and soul into his oratory. One observer recalled, "He had a freewheeling body.... Head, hair, arms, shoulders—everything [moved] in a different direction."

Long embraces two close Louisiana colleagues, Public Service Commissioner James O'Connor (left) and Governor Oscar K. Allen.

SENATE FILIBUSTERS

In addition to his fiery rhetoric Huey Long's speaking skills included an ability to talk for long periods, whether people wanted to hear him or not. In 1933, faced with the Republican-backed Banking Act, the senator jumped into the national spotlight with a successful filibuster that lasted three weeks. Two years later he engaged in the second-longest Senate filibuster ever.

Long staged this second filibuster because he feared that some of his political opponents from Louisiana might become senior members of the National Recovery Administration (NRA), the organization established by Roosevelt to promote business recovery during the Depression. To block these appointments, Long therefore supported a provision requiring Senate confirmation of the positions. Despite Roosevelt's opposition to the proposal, Long tried to force Senate Democrats to approve it. Standing before his

The Share-Our-Wealth Program

Huey Long launched his Share-Our-Wealth Society in January 1934. Then, on February 5, he entered into the Congressional Record a paper that he termed his "appeal to the people of America." Called *Carry Out the Command of the Lord,* the paper began: "People of America: In every community get together at once and organize a share-our-wealth society—Motto: Every man a king."

The Share-Our-Wealth platform laid out by Long had seven main principles:

"1. To limit poverty by providing that every deserving family shall share in the wealth of America for not less than one-third of the average wealth, thereby to possess not less than $5,000 free of debt.

"2. To limit fortunes to such a few million dollars as will allow the balance of the American people to share in the wealth and profits of the land.

"3. Old-age pensions of $30 per month to persons over 60 years of age who do not earn as much as $1,000 per year or who possess less than $10,000 in cash or property, thereby to remove from the field of labor in times of unemployment those who have contributed their share to the public service.

"4. To limit the hours of work to such an extent as to prevent overproduction and to give the workers of America some share in the recreations, conveniences, and luxuries of life.

"5. To balance agricultural production with what can be sold and consumed according to the laws of God, which have never failed.

"6. To care for the veterans of our wars.

"7. Taxation to run the Government to be supported, first, by reducing big fortunes from the top, thereby to improve the country and provide employment in public works whenever agricultural surplus is such as to render unnecessary, in whole or in part, any particular crop."

Huey Long replies to General Hugh Johnson, one-time director of Roosevelt's National Recovery Administration (NRA). The general was a regular critic of Long's politics and plans.

fellow legislators on June 12, he picked up a copy of the U.S. Constitution and started analyzing it, point by laborious point.

After several hours many senators were napping. Long asked that they be forced to listen to him. Vice President John Nance Garner dismissed this request as "unusual cruelty under the Bill of Rights." Long continued, answering questions passed to him by reporters in the press gallery, and then proceeded to offer his recipe for potlikkers and fried oysters, Louisiana-style. Wrapping up at 4:00 A.M., his total intervention lasted 15 hours and 30 minutes. His proposal was defeated.

LOUISIANA BUSINESS

Long was stirring up the nation's capital, but he was not neglecting business back in Louisiana.

During his term as senator he procured funding to expand Louisiana State University (LSU) and to undertake massive highway construction in the state. From 1934 to 1935 he further consolidated his grip on politics in the state by closing local offices. In this way Long almost wiped out local government and gave himself the power to appoint all state workers. What was left of Louisiana's critical press faced censorship (see box, page 50).

LONG, ROOSEVELT, AND THE NEW DEAL

Despite making his presence there strongly felt, Long was generally uninterested in the Senate. He saw the office of senator as a way of promoting his own national agenda and of lobbying Roosevelt about his own, highly radical social programs. From the beginning Long had made clear his belief in the redistribution of the nation's wealth. He supported Roosevelt at the 1932 Democratic Convention, campaigned for him during the presidential elections, then worked energetically with the newly elected president in support of his New Deal (see Volume 2, Chapter 1, "The Election of 1932," and Chapter 2, "The First Hundred Days").

Long grew disillusioned with Roosevelt's policies, which he began to consider barely distinguishable from those of his predecessor, Herbert Hoover. He voiced his doubts openly, saying: "The Roosevelt depression debt is $9 billion more than the Hoover depression debt; the unemployment under Roosevelt has eclipsed everything Hoover ever heard about…."

For Long the New Deal simply did not go far enough. It was not attacking what he saw as the core problem: unequally distributed wealth. In "Roosevelt's depression" the rich were getting richer and the poor poorer. The New Deal was failing to break up great fortunes, while mass unemployment and indebtedness continued among the poor. By 1933 Long had become one of the president's harshest critics. In a radio address later entered into the Congressional Record on January 14, 1935, he attacked the president again: "[Roosevelt] admits that most of the people of America are impoverished because the rich people have all the money. He says they ought not to allow them to have it all, but in the next breath he gives out a statement that the big rich must not be taxed very much, and that is as far as we ever get with him. He rode into the President's office on the platform of redistributing wealth. He has done no such thing and has made no effort to do any such thing since he has been there."

SHARE-OUR-WEALTH

Since Roosevelt was unwilling to accept his plans for wealth redistribution, Long set out to achieve his own goals. What he was doing in Louisiana was just the start of what he hoped to do in the nation as a whole. Just as he loathed Louisiana's rich aristocracy, so Long despised the privilege and

This 1933 caricature compares Long (foreground) with European dictators Hitler, Mussolini, and Stalin. All are dressed as Napoleon.

power of national magnates like J. P. Morgan, J. D. Rockefeller, and Andrew Mellon. He was willing to apply to them the same sorts of confiscatory taxes and monopoly-busting measures that he had used in his home state. As he said in the first of his autobiographies: "I had come to the United States Senate with only one project in mind, which was that by every means of action and persuasion I might do something to spread the wealth of the land among all of the people."

Long had been calling for the rich to "share the wealth" for many years. In January 1934 he finally gave his appeal a name and a form by founding the Share-Our-Wealth Society. Long's program (see box, page 52) proposed taxing the rich highly and redistributing the proceeds among ordinary Americans. They were to receive both a guaranteed family income of

What's in a Name?

Huey Long's character earned him a variety of nicknames. His dictatorial tendencies led to "Tinpot Napoleon" and "Bonaparte of the Bayous." The comparison was with Napoleon I Bonaparte, the emperor of France from 1804 to 1815. Artist Miguel Covarrubias, who drew the cartoon above, also made this connection. Long's most famous nickname, the Kingfish, came from the *Amos 'n' Andy* radio show. In his drawing Covarrubias has adorned Long's hat with an image of the fish. Today the term "kingfish" can be used more generally to mean any powerful leader.

Huey Long stands outside the door to Roosevelt's offices in 1933. By this time Long was already nursing his own ambitions to be president.

"the Lord prescribed" the last, which would stop any person becoming too rich or too poor.

Long's plan included limiting family fortunes to a few million dollars and inheritances to one million. In addition, no family would be allowed to earn more than $1 million annually. Tax revenues would be used for large public works projects, for education subsidies, and for distribution to poor families, in order to keep them from sliding into abject poverty. "At worst," Long said, "a family could have a fairly comfortable home, an automobile, and a radio, with other reasonable home conveniences, and a place to educate their children." Furthermore, he reasoned that if work hours were reduced, everyone could have a job and share in the earnings.

Long's beliefs earned him many enemies. Hodding Carter, liberal editor of the *Hammond Courier* and an outspoken anti-Long watchdog, warned the nation of Long's history of power abuses. In a 1935 essay he dismissed the Share-Our-Wealth plan as one that "makes of poverty a rallying point, political and economic, about which Huey Long can work toward a national goal that is by no means so hazy as are his wealth-sharing nostrums for making everybody prosperous." Carter also attacked Long's plans as impracticable. In addition, many statisticians of the day cast serious doubt on Long's claim that a confiscatory tax on the rich would be enough to provide every poor American with several thousand dollars.

SHARE-OUR-WEALTH CLUBS

Huey Long's wish to end the concentration of wealth in the hands of a small minority led him to introduce three controversial bills in Congress. However,

$2,000 to $3,000 every year and also a debt-free $5,000 "homestead" allowance.

By Long's estimation nearly half of the money in U.S. banks was in the hands of 0.1 percent of the population; 66 percent of the American people did not even have bank accounts. His lowest estimate was that 85 percent of the nation's wealth was in the hands of just 4 percent of the people. He believed that the United States had a choice of three fates: rule by financial masters, or a type of modern feudalism; Communism; or a share-the-wealth society. He believed

In this 1935 cartoon Roosevelt is haunted by multiple Huey Longs. Its caption reads: "The goblins'll get you if you don't look out!"

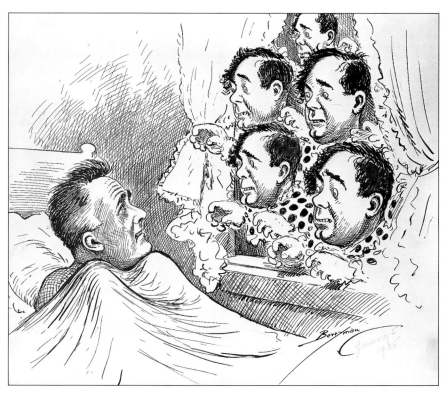

Reverend Gerald Smith

Huey Long was not alone in his charisma and gift for public speaking. Another dynamic figure who loudly supported his wealth redistribution plans was the Reverend Gerald L. K. Smith, a radical, red-headed minister from the Disciples of Christ church. Smith was the "high priest and prophet of Senator Long's Share-Our-Wealth movement." Turning his fire-and-brimstone religious language toward the preaching of prosperity for ordinary Americans, Smith for a short time traveled the United States spreading Long's message in words like these:

"Let's pull down these huge piles of gold until there shall be a real job, not a little old sow-belly, black-eyed pea job but a real spending money, beefsteak and gravy, Chevrolet, Ford in the garage, new suit, Thomas Jefferson, Jesus Christ, red, white, and blue job for every man!... Lift us out of this wretchedness, O Lord, out of this poverty, lift us who stand in slavery tonight. Rally us under this young man who came out of...north Louisiana, who leads us like a Moses out of the land of bondage into the land of milk and honey where every man is a king but no man wears a crown. Amen."

although he added color and flair to Congressional debate, Long proved an ineffectual legislator at the national level. His true sphere of action was among ordinary people, and he broke new ground by buying radio time from the National Broadcasting Company (NBC) to take his message directly to them. For Long Share-the-Wealth was more than a suggestion to Congress. It was a movement he hoped would spread like wildfire among Americans, and he appealed openly to them to make this happen: "I ask somebody in every city, town, village, and farm community of America to take this as my personal request to call a meeting of as many neighbors and friends as will come to it to start a share-our-wealth society. Elect a president and a secretary and charge no dues."

Share-Our-Wealth clubs began to pop up nationwide. The down-and-out flocked to hear Long and other rousing speakers. In any one gathering as many as 500 new converts would sign up for the

•

"I ask somebody in every...community... to start a share-our-wealth society."

•

National Share-Our-Wealth Society. Membership was free, partly because, as Long explained, "if any such thing as dues were collected from members for such expenses, the thieves of Wall Street and their newspapers and radio liars would immediately say that I had a scheme to get money." Joining was as simple as filling out an application with one's name, age, address, and the names and addresses of other potential members. In return new members received a card emblazoned with the slogan "Share-Our-Wealth Society—Every Man a King."

Each new member had the chance to become secretary or

even president of a local club. This could be achieved by getting two or more neighbors to fill out cards and send them to Washington. On Sundays and holidays members held Share-Our-Wealth parades, complete with U.S. flags and banners. Local club leaders often emulated the flamboyant speeches of Long and his lieutenants.

By 1935 Long supporters had founded 27,000 Share-Our-Wealth Clubs, claiming as many as eight million members. Later historians have found it difficult to gauge how committed and how involved in the cause many of those members were.

REACHING THE PEOPLE
As Huey Long's influence grew, he became a frequent presence on national radio. Like Roosevelt with his regular fireside chats, Long used the medium with great effectiveness. He did not stop at radio talks, speeches, and books to get his message across. In 1935 Long joined Castro Carrazo, band director at Louisiana State University, to compose a Share-

Our-Wealth song. The result, "Every Man a King," was performed by Ina Ray Hutton and Her All-Girl Orchestra:

Why weep or slumber America
Land of brave and true
With castles and clothing
and food for all
All belongs to you
Ev'ry man a King,
ev'ry man a King
For you can be a millionaire
But there's something
belonging to others
There's enough for all
people to share
When it's sunny June and
December too
Or in the Winter time or Spring
There'll be peace without end
Ev'ry neighbor a friend
With ev'ry man a King

Long proclaimed that should he ever seek the presidency, this

Roosevelt Retaliates

As the presidential election of 1936 approached, Roosevelt and his political adviser Jim Farley set out to undermine Huey Long's appeal to the public. Their tactics included openly investigating the Senator's tax affairs for irregularities and spotlighting the highly dictatorial nature of his rule over Louisiana. In addition the administration suspended many building projects in Long's home state that were run by the Public Works Administration (PWA), the New Deal agency set up to finance construction work.

anthem would become one of his main campaign songs. He also promised to make Carrazo director of the Marine Band.

SEEKING THE PRESIDENCY

In August 1935 Huey Long announced his intention to challenge Franklin D. Roosevelt in the presidential elections of the following year. That Long wanted to be president of the United States was hardly a secret. His optimistic 146-page book *My First Days in the White House* (1935) outlined the progress of a hypothetical Long administration in seven detailed chapters: Wherein a New President Takes Office and Outlines a Program to Share Our Wealth; Wherein We Arrange to

Louisiana voters began using tire covers like this in early 1935. They fully expected that their man would run for president the next year.

Overhaul and Revive the Nation; Wherein We Care for the Soul and Body of a Great Nation; Wherein the New President Encounters the Masters of Finance and Destiny; Wherein the Masters of Finance are Ours; Wherein Rebellion Brews and Fades; Wherein We Inspect the Revived and Greater America.

This "second autobiography" is a fanciful tale. Former political enemies and great financiers alike fall at Long's feet and support the Share-Our-Wealth program. President Long condescends to former opponents, appointing Roosevelt secretary of the navy and Herbert Hoover secretary of commerce. J. D. Rockefeller gives up all but $5 million of his wealth and joins other billionaires to help Long revive America.

The result of this extraordinary transformation is a nation at work, but with plenty of leisure time. Health care is available to all. President Long is everywhere

This game from a 1936 magazine depicts a make-believe race for the White House. The participants shown are Long and Roosevelt.

Long makes a radio broadcast in 1935. The medium served him well by enabling him to speak directly to the ordinary American public.

greeted by cheering crowds, and the world looks to America for inspiration. In Long's imaginings foreign countries send emissaries and statisticians to explore the revived country. He does not have the time to see them all but hands out the following general advice: "For all I have not told you, the whole explanation is in the Bible."

TOWNSEND AND COUGHLIN

Long was far from achieving the success of his dreams, but his message was catching on among certain segments of the American

•

"For all I have not told you, the whole explanation is in the Bible."

•

population. He was not the only person asking for the common man's piece of the pie. The Share-Our-Wealth clubs were one part of a growing populist movement lobbying Roosevelt for much more radical reforms.

Another influential member of this movement was Dr. Francis E. Townsend. In 1934 he set up the Old-Age Revolving Pension Plan, generally called the Townsend Plan, to push for $200 monthly pensions for people over 60 years of age. Like Share-Our-Wealth clubs, Townsend Clubs grew up across the United States, their membership rising from 500,000 in 1934 to two million by 1935. The passage of the Social Security Act on August 14, 1935 (see Chapter 5, "Welfare"), removed some of the Townsendites' momentum, but they remained a formidable political action group for several years afterward.

Father Charles E. Coughlin, a radical Roman Catholic priest with a large following on national radio, had stirred up his own populist

A black family outside their house on a Louisiana bayou. Long sought to improve the lives of poor people like these, whatever their race.

movement. Once an ardent Roosevelt supporter, he had since joined Long in his hatred of the president's policies and the slow progress of reform. Coughlin's increasingly political broadcasts attacked international bankers, Wall Street, the gold standard, labor unions, and Communists. They also became highly anti-Semitic. In 1934 Coughlin set up the National Union for Social Justice, which challenged New Deal policies and advocated nationalizing banks, natural resources, and utilities.

Since Long had the potential support of all the disgruntled Americans who followed both Townsend and Coughlin, many people considered him a real threat to Roosevelt's chances of reelection. The president himself called Long "one of the two most dangerous men in America." The other, in his view, was World War I veteran General Douglas MacArthur.

Faced with Long's expected push for the White House, the Democratic National Committee conducted a secret poll to measure what threat he posed. Long's national organization was found to be not only poorly organized, but also too decentralized and largely ineffectual at forming alliances with similar movements. It was nonetheless concluded that if Long ran on a third-party ticket in the 1936 presidential elections, he might gain up to 11 percent of the popular vote. This would not be anywhere near enough to win him the election, but it could certainly spoil Roosevelt's chances for a second term in office.

In March 1935 Roosevelt supporters made their first counterattack against Long and Coughlin. Former director of the National Recovery Administration (NRA) Hugh Johnson spoke out against their ideas at a dinner held in his honor. The speech provoked a whirlwind of debate about the New Deal and the opposing populist plans. In order to curtail the rise to power of both Long and

A man sells the Social Justice *newspaper in New York City. The paper was founded by the populist priest Father Charles E. Coughlin.*

Coughlin, Roosevelt himself was also obliged to move further leftward, toward the so-called "Second New Deal."

ASSASSINATION AND AFTER

A month after announcing that he would run for president, Long returned to Baton Rouge to oversee a special session of the state legislature. There were many issues on the agenda, of which the most relevant would prove to be legislation designed to broaden Long's power by gerrymandering the district of Judge Benjamin Davy, a long-time political enemy.

On September 8, 1935, as Long walked down the marble corridor of the state capitol that he had helped build, Dr. Carl A. Weiss, a local physician, stepped out from behind a pillar and shot him. Weiss was Judge Davy's son-in-law. Witnesses said they saw Weiss walk up as if to greet Long, only to shoot him in the abdomen

at close range with a pistol. As Long floundered down the hall yelling, bodyguards shot and killed Weiss, leaving two bullet holes in his head, 30 in the front of his body, and 29 in his back.

One of Long's associates found the injured senator in a stairwell and had him rushed to Our Lady of the Lake Sanitarium. There, Dr. Arthur Vidrine discovered that the assailant's bullet had entered the upper right part of Long's abdomen and come out through his back. Since two expert sur-

geons summoned from New Orleans were stuck in traffic, Vidrine had to operate to keep the senator from bleeding to death. When the surgeons did arrive, Long was too weak to face another operation. Long is said to have talked politics to the last. "God, don't let me die!" he reportedly cried from his deathbed, "I have so much to do!" He died on September 10, 1935, at 4:06 A.M., and was buried on the state capitol grounds in Baton Rouge.

A family car at a 1936 rally in favor of the Townsend Plan. The Plan had millions of supporters all across the United States.

4. LONG'S LEGACY

Long's political machine was far from dead. Rose McConnell Long took her late husband's place in the U.S. Senate for the remainder of his term, until 1937. Long's son Russell also followed in his footsteps, serving in the U.S. Senate from 1948 until his retirement in 1986. Other Long relatives to enter politics included two of Huey's brothers. George S. Long was a member of the U.S. House of Representatives from 1953 to 1958; Earl K. Long was

acting governor of Louisiana from 1939 to 1940, and governor from 1948 to 1952 and 1956 to 1960.

After Long's death his many followers continued to support his ideals, in particular pushing for the expansion of Louisiana's public sector. Long was also remembered in a personal way: Some poor

These holes mark the marble of the Louisiana State Capitol near where Long was shot. They may have been made by the bullets that killed him.

Louisianans took "Huey Long" as their middle names. However, the involvement of the Long political machine in a series of scandals led to the election of Sam Houston Jones as Louisiana governor in 1940. He served until 1944.

DIFFERING VIEWS

The opinions expressed about Long after his death varied. Jones' assessment of his predecessor was not flattering: "Nothing like the regime of Huey Long has ever been enacted on American soil before. Only a patriot of the staunchest character could stand up to the power of Huey and the threats and reprisals which he used so freely. Those who were willing to do so paralleled the acts of America's bravest patriots at any stage of American history." Some people, however, defended Long's rule as a necessary evil in difficult times. "His opponents called him a dictator, but Long's behavior had the approval of the

voters," according to historian Robert C. Byrd. "During that terrible period of depression, they wanted strong leadership, and Long was offering it."

THE 1936 ELECTION

Despite the sudden loss of its leader, the "Share-Our-Wealth" movement marched forward. Gerald L. K. Smith (see box, page 55) led the movement after Long's death, though his controversial character and alleged sympathies with fascism soon brought his tenure to an end. In a third-party attempt to break the grip of the Democrats and Republicans, Smith joined both Dr. Francis E. Townsend and Father Charles E. Coughlin to found the Union Party. With Long gone, however, the new party lacked a willing and able candidate for the presidential election of 1936.

The lack of leadership did not bother Gerald Smith. In a speech

Dr. Carl A. Weiss, the assassin who brought Long's political career to a violent end. The photograph was taken a month before the shooting.

to Coughlin's National Union of Social Justice Convention in Cleveland, Ohio, he proclaimed: "These great phenomenal assemblies, whether they be headed by Dr. Francis E. Townsend, Gerald Smith, or Father Charles E. Coughlin, represent the unmistakable edict that is being issued to the corrupt, seething politicians… that the…god-fearing American people are about to take over the U.S. Government of America!"

The Union Party eventually selected William Lemke, a little-known Republican congressman from North Dakota, to run for office on their behalf. Thomas C. O'Brien, a labor lawyer from Boston, was nominated for vice president. Some observers, while far from predicting a Union Party victory, did still believe that the radical coalition could steal many Democratic votes from Roosevelt. In fact, however, Lemke failed even to get on the ballot in some states. On election day Roosevelt won a landslide victory over the Republican challenger Alf Landon, winning 61 percent of the vote (see

The Long Legend

Huey Long survived not only in the power structure that he created, but also in legend and literature. The novelist, poet, and critic Robert Penn Warren, who was also Professor of English at Louisiana State University from 1934 to 1942, immortalized Long in a novel. *All the King's Men* (1946) depicted the rise to power of fiery politician Willie Stark, who strongly resembled Long. Stark's stormy life, which ended in sudden assassination, also closely mirrored that of the Louisiana senator. *All the King's Men* earned instant acclaim, winning the Pulitzer Prize in the year of its publication.

The assassination scene from the Columbia motion picture of All the King's Men *(1949).*

Three years later Penn's novel was made into a major motion picture by Columbia. The picture, which starred Broderick Crawford as Stark, gained mixed reviews, bu won Crawford a best-acting Oscar. One review, written for the *New Yorker* magazine by the famous critic Pauline Kael, proclaimed: "Broderick Crawford's Willie Stark might just make you feel better about the President you've got...."

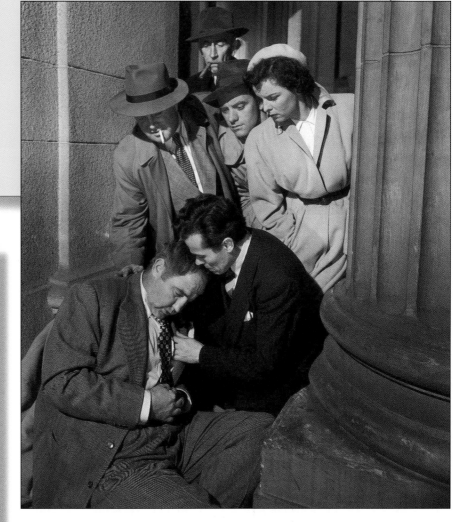

Volume 2, Chapter 6, "The Election of 1936").

The Union Party won just 2 percent of the vote and had no representatives in the electoral college. Coughlin dissolved the Union Party four days later. While many Americans had voiced their support for Townsend, Coughlin, and Long, it had become clear they were not necessarily opposed to Roosevelt's New Deal.

THE RIGHT-WING BACKLASH

The flood of New Deal legislation during the early days of President Roosevelt's time in office enjoyed widespread support. But approval was by no means unanimous, and in time conservative forces mounted fierce resistance.

General Electric president Gerard Swope seated (left) beside Henry Ford. Swope favored cooperation between business and government.

When Franklin D. Roosevelt entered the White House in March 1933, he had no intention that his administration should find itself in conflict with the powers of finance, banking, and big business (see Volume 2, Chapter 2, "The First Hundred Days"). What he wanted, and foresaw, was cooperation between government and business, a partnership working together for the benefit of the nation. Self-regulation and a recognition of the larger issues facing America were what he expected from the industrial and financial magnates.

Roosevelt was not alone in wanting this business–government partnership (see Volume 5, Chapter 1, "Government, Industry, and Economic Policy"). Several influential businessmen, including the president of General Electric and the chairman of the United States Chamber of Commerce, spoke of the need for cooperation to combat the Great Depression. The comparison often made was

(see Volume 1, Chapter 2, "The United States in World War I").

with the position in World War I Then, government and business had cooperated in the face of a national crisis. The Great Depression was a crisis on the same scale as war, and the same cooperation was required.

Not enough people in the business world were so far-seeing, however, and the measures that Roosevelt's administration took inevitably brought it into confrontation with businessmen and financiers. In his first term in office Roosevelt came to the conclusion that self-regulation would not work because industry did not want it to work. In other words, the business community as a whole would sacrifice the larger national interest to its own short-term goals. "I get more and more convinced," Roosevelt said, "that most of them can't see farther than the next dividend."

As he saw industrialists openly flouting or evading government regulations and pouring millions into campaigns that portrayed him and his administration as communist or worse, his will to force through reform, with or without the cooperation of industry and

Secretary of the Treasury William Woodin looks on as the president signs the Emergency Banking Act into law, March 9, 1933.

On March 3, 1933, the eve of President Roosevelt's inauguration, the long-running banking crisis triggered a run on the banks.

finance, was strengthened. By 1935 Roosevelt was markedly more distrustful of the business world, and his inner circle of advisers and policy-makers included many more who were antitrust and anti-big business.

1. NEW DEAL AGENDA

The day after he was sworn in as president, Roosevelt called a special session of Congress and proclaimed a four-day national bank holiday starting on March 6. This was an emergency measure to cope with the run on the banks by millions of panicky depositors, which had begun the day before his inauguration. This session of the 73rd Congress had strong Democrat majorities in both houses. It passed a torrent of legislation, and this period became known as the First Hundred Days, in which the scope of Roosevelt's New Deal was revealed.

The first action of the special session was the Emergency Banking Act of March 9. By the terms of this act the President was given broad new powers over credit transactions and those in currency, gold, silver, and foreign currency. Gold hoarding and the exportation of gold were later prohibited, and the U.S. was taken off the gold standard for its currency. Most important in the short term, Roosevelt's swift actions in declaring the bank holiday and in passing the act restored people's confidence. When banks did reopen, the

disorganization of industry, which burdens interstate and foreign commerce, affects the public welfare, and undermines the standards of living of the American people, is hereby declared to exist." The NIRA was seen by the administration as the cornerstone of its program to combat that national emergency and to set the nation back on its economic feet. Roosevelt viewed it as an expression of business–government cooperation, a renewal of the wartime pact he remembered. He made this explicit as he signed it into law on June 16, 1933. "Many good men," he said, "voted this new charter with misgiving. I do not share

panic had subsided, and people, in fact, began to deposit more money than was withdrawn. Fourteen major pieces of legislation followed the Emergency Banking Act, from the Economy Act, enacted on March 15, to the National Industrial Recovery Act (NIRA), enacted on June 16, and were swept through Congress. "More history has been made during these 15 weeks than in any other comparable peacetime period," one observer noted.

The NIRA and the NRA

The preamble to the NIRA made it clear how the administration saw the state of the nation as Roosevelt's first term began. "A national emergency," it ran, "productive of widespread unemployment and

Secretary of the Interior Harold Ickes takes a direct hand in a slum-clearance project in Atlanta, Georgia, in 1934.

Oil derricks at Venice, California, in 1933. That summer the oil industry joined other major industries in agreeing to NRA codes of practice.

these doubts. I had part in the great cooperation of 1917 and 1918, and it is my faith that we can count on our industry once more to join in our general purpose to lift this new threat."

The focus of the NIRA was twofold, on public spending and on industry self-regulation. To deal with public spending, it established the Public Works Administration (PWA), funded with $3.3 billion and charged with the supervision of the building of roads, public buildings, and other projects (see Volume 2, Chapter 5, "Putting People to Work"). Secretary of the Interior Harold Ickes (1874–1952) was appointed director of the PWA.

To create industry self-regulation and to balance the interests of business and labor, the NIRA initiated a bold new strategy. A

Wartime Cooperation

When President Roosevelt harked back to the spirit of cooperation between industry and labor during World War I, he was thinking of such agencies as the War Labor Policies Board. Established by President Wilson in May 1918, it was empowered to regulate wages and hours and to provide central direction to the work force. The support of organized labor, which was vital to the war effort, was gained by such measures.

board composed of both business and labor leaders in each industry would draw up a code for that industry that would govern prices,

wages, work hours, production limits, and so on.

The National Recovery Administration (NRA) was established to put this aspect of the NIRA into practice. To head the NRA, and to undertake the central task of negotiating fair competition codes and agreements, Roosevelt appointed Hugh Johnson (1882–1942). Johnson was an ex-army brigadier-general who had shown his administrative abilities in World War I. On the country's entry into the war in 1917 he had helped formulate the plans for selective service in the Army and had been involved in the administration of the draft. Since the war he had worked in business. Roosevelt saw him as a man who combined knowledge of the business world with the tough, no-nonsense approach of the military.

Johnson's most pressing job in the summer of 1933 was to get NRA code agreements with all the major industries. He was aware that it was a Herculean and thank-

An NRA poster with the Blue Eagle that became such a familiar symbol of the New Deal. Its display showed compliance with the code.

less task. In a book published after he left the NRA he called it "like mounting the guillotine on the infinitesimal gamble that the ax won't work."

The nation's 10 leading industries were steel, shipbuilding, oil, woolens, electricals, cotton, the garment industry, automobiles, lumber, and soft coal. Johnson needed leaders of these industries to accept codes of practice. Only the cotton industry made immediate arrangements to agree to such basics as maximum hours and minimum wages. The others held out against committing themselves to any NRA-mediated regulation.

The Blue Eagle

In a brilliant propaganda coup Johnson launched the Blue Eagle campaign to get individual employers to pledge directly to the president that their companies would uphold standards on wages and hours. It was a clever appeal to patriotism and to a national interest overriding sectarian interests. Very rapidly the campaign gathered momentum, and its symbol—the Blue Eagle— could be seen on everything from the pages of newspapers to the displays in store windows. The campaign's motto, "We Do Our Part," became a familiar one. In a parade in New York to support the Blue Eagle campaign 250,000 people marched down Fifth Avenue, singing and waving placards. Eventually more than two million employers made the pledge to Roosevelt.

Johnson had outfoxed the leaders of the major industries, and he was now able to return to the offensive to get their names on codes of practice. By early August 1933 shipbuilding, woolens, electricals, and the garment industry had come on board, and they were swiftly followed by oil, steel, and lumber, although Johnson had to make major concessions to these powerful employers. By the end of August all the automobile manufacturers, with the exception of the stubbornly rejectionist Henry Ford, had made an agreement with the NRA. The high-water mark of Johnson's achievements with the NRA came on September 18, 1933, when the last of the major industrial groups,

the soft-coal operators, put their names to a code. In only three months Johnson, through a combination of energy, bluster, and sophisticated tactical thinking, had brought all the major industries together, for the first time, in a series of agreements about industrial relations and conditions.

By the following summer, however, the NRA was under attack

•

"Like mounting the guillotine on the… gamble that the ax won't work."

•

from all sides, and even its closest supporters were doubting its effectiveness. It was blamed by many for driving up prices. Small businesses complained that they were being shackled by too much bureaucracy and paperwork. This was a theme taken up by many of Roosevelt's critics, including the maverick and flamboyant Louisiana Senator Huey Long (1893–1935), who quipped that it would "take 40 lawyers to tell a shoeshine stand how to operate and be certain he didn't go to jail" (see Chapter 3, "Huey Long").

The NRA had opened itself to criticism by attempting to regulate relatively unimportant targets like the dog food industry and the shoulder pad manufacturing industry. It had, however, prevented abuses and exploitation of labor in small businesses, which may, as much as bureaucracy, have made it the target of their criticism.

The National Industrial Recovery Act had, with the best of

intentions, muddied the waters of labor relations by guaranteeing workers, through its controversial Section 7(a), the right to collective bargaining, but had not provided an effective means of resolving disputes (see Chapter 6, "The Unionization of Labor"). The employers, resentful of what they saw as interference in their ability to manage their workforce, proved regularly uncompromising in negotiations with unions.

The promise of Section 7(a) had inspired numerous union-organizing drives, and the fall of 1933 had seen a succession of bitter strikes to force recognition of unions in the coal and steel industries. These, and others, continued throughout 1934. In that year more than 1.5 million workers had walked off their jobs in more than 1,400 disputes.

Removing Hugh Johnson

To add to the beleaguered position of the NRA, its head, Hugh Johnson, was increasingly seen as a loose cannon. He was a heavy drinker and a volatile personality.

After a series of private arguments with colleagues and public gaffes in speeches he was removed from his position in August and replaced by a five-man board. The most influential voice on the board was that of lawyer Donald Richberg, who tended to support the claims of business. All of these problems with the NRA, however, became of secondary importance in the spring of 1935 when it came under assault from the Supreme Court.

From the moment of first entering office, Roosevelt and his close colleagues had been anxious about the Supreme Court and its power to derail legislation through its decisions (see Chapter 2, "The Supreme Court"). Liberal justices such as Louis Brandeis, Benjamin Cardozo, and Harlan Fiske Stone were more than outweighed by the four members of the bench—McReynolds, Sutherland, Van Devanter, and Butler—who were

Richard Whitney, president of the New York Stock Exchange, takes an oath before the Senate Banking and Currency Committee in 1933.

dyed-in-the-wool conservatives. Between the liberals and the conservatives were Chief Justice Charles Evans Hughes and Owen Roberts.

THE SUPREME COURT AND THE NRA

In the early months of 1935 a number of majority decisions by the Court went against the government without inflicting significant damage to it. Ironically, the decision that threatened the very continuation of the New Deal was a unanimous one. On May 27, 1935, the ruling in the case of *A. L. A. Schechter Poultry Corp. et al. v. United States* effectively rendered the NRA unconstitutional. The previous year the Schechter brothers, poultry traders and shippers from New York, had been found guilty of a number of breaches of the "Live Poultry Code" established by Johnson's

A poster celebrating the 45th anniversary of the Social Security Act of 1935, one of the most effective and durable New Deal measures.

NRA and signed off by Roosevelt. On reexamination of the case the Supreme Court questioned the constitutional basis for the prosecution of the Schechters and went on to find that their business was an intrastate one. As such, the federal government could not legally regulate it. The ruling was a body blow to the NRA and by extension a severe criticism of the New Deal.

Roosevelt was astonished by the decision and by the fact that justices like Cardozo and Brandeis agreed with their conservative colleagues. For some time the president had been wavering between those advisers recommending caution and those, like Harvard professor Felix Frankfurter (1882–1965), who argued that the attempt at cooperation with big business had clearly failed.

•

"The most influential single individual in the United States."

•

Frankfurter, who had fought in the 1920s to save Sacco and Vanzetti from execution and was to be appointed a Supreme Court justice by Roosevelt in 1939, was a man of great influence at the White House. Hugh Johnson once described him, with slight exaggeration, as "the most influential single individual in the United States." The government–business partnership, Frankfurter claimed, was dead and should be buried. Roosevelt should face up to the fact that business, particularly the giant holding companies, was the enemy of his New Deal, and no progress could be made without a direct confrontation with it.

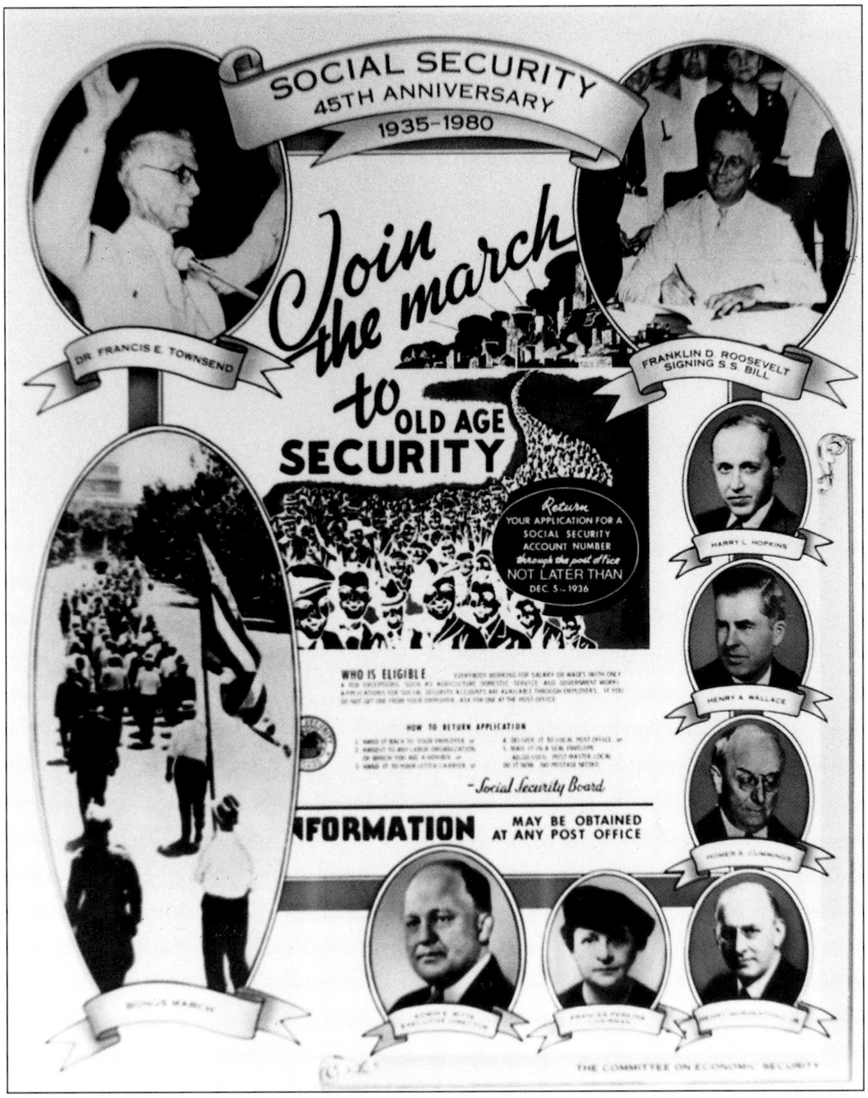

2. FDR FIGHTS BACK

Early in May Frankfurter wrote to his intellectual mentor Louis Brandeis, "If only Business could become still more articulate in its true feelings toward FDR so that even his genial habits would see the futility of hoping anything from Business in 1936." Now Roosevelt did seem to have woken up to the fact that Frankfurter was right, and, ironically, it was a judgment of the Supreme Court on which Brandeis sat that had pushed him. In the wake of the Supreme Court decision Roosevelt was to relaunch the New Deal program.

In the mass of legislation that was undertaken in the First Hundred Days there were important acts that helped shape the administration's relationship with the financial world. The Glass-Steagall Banking Act, enacted on June 16, 1933, was one. It created the Federal Deposit Insurance Corporation, which could guarantee bank deposits up to $2,500, later raised to $5,000. It also provided for savings and industrial banks becoming members of the Federal

Waiting for a relief check in California. The WPA created five million jobs by 1938, much reducing the public relief roles.

Reserve System and, by separating commercial banking from investment banking, dealt with the problem of banks speculating with depositors' funds. The Securities Act, adopted in late May 1933, was another, and it may have sent out perhaps the first clear signal to the business community that the New Deal might work against what they saw as their best interests.

REGULATING THE STOCK EXCHANGE

To draft the Securities and Exchange Act Roosevelt called on two of the most able of Felix Frankfurter's protégés from Harvard Law School, Tom Corcoran (1900–1981) and Benjamin Cohen (1894–1983). The act was intended to reduce the amount of investment fraud taking place by obliging all companies to register new issues of stocks and bonds with the Federal Trade Commission. "It will not hurt any honest seller of securities," Roosevelt wrote; but this kind of federal intervention in financial markets had few precedents, and many bankers and financiers criticized it.

Still intent on soothing the feelings of business, Roosevelt postponed any further exchange regulation. He was wary of the bitter reactions to it that were almost bound to occur. However, in February 1934 he sent a bill to Congress that gave further powers to the Federal Trade Commission. Once again drafted by Corcoran and Cohen, the bill was a major move toward federal regulation of the stock market.

It established a new Securities and Exchange Commission (the

first chairman of the commission, when it came into operation, was to be Joseph P. Kennedy, father of the future president), which was given the power to license stock exchanges and to enforce rules to protect the interests of shareholders. The aim was, as Roosevelt acknowledged, to restrict the use of exchanges "for purely speculative purposes."

Protest from the market was immediate and hard-hitting. Richard Whitney, the president of the New York Stock Exchange, was, at first, coldly and superciliously dismissive. "You gentlemen are making a great mistake," he informed the administration, "The Exchange is a perfect institution." Later he presided over the establishment of committees opposed to the bill and moved to Washington to direct the battle against it. (Whitney's campaign was brought to a juddering halt when he was convicted of grand larceny and

sent to Sing Sing.) The bill also brought many businessmen, such as the chairman of Sears Roebuck, Robert Wood, who had previously been supporters of the New Deal, into the ranks of its opponents.

Roosevelt was still eager to appease these opponents as much as possible, and at the beginning of March he asked Corcoran and Cohen to look at the Securities and Exchange Act again. They made changes in some of its more stringent clauses, but the revised bill met with just as much opposition as the original.

James Rand, the chairman of Remington Rand, in a statement to the House Commerce Committee, raised what was becoming a familiar complaint against the New Deal. He said that the bill represented a step "down the road from democracy to communism." By now, however, the president was unwilling to yield further ground, and the bill passed through both

•

"It will not hurt any honest seller of securities."

•

houses in May and was signed by him on June 6, 1934. The Securities Exchange Act was now law.

The Supreme Court ruling in the Schechter case in May 1935 marked the end of the NRA, judged to be unconstitutional. With it went much of the foundation of the New Deal. However, the NRA was already losing credibility when it ran foul of the Supreme Court, and the ruling was the signal not for retrenchment by the Roosevelt administration but

Labor's Champion

German-born Robert F. Wagner represented New York in the U.S. Senate from 1927 (see box, page 91). He was a political ally of Al Smith's, but enjoyed a good working relationship with Roosevelt. As well as masterminding the labor relations act that bears his name, Wagner was responsible for the passage of a public housing bill in 1937. Until retiring from the Senate in 1949, he remained a leading liberal voice in the Democratic Party.

for a renewed program of legislation. As early as his annual address to Congress on January 4, 1935, Roosevelt had outlined what he and his advisers envisaged as the second phase of the New Deal, in which a program of social and tax reforms was to be rolled out. Now it was time to put that second phase into action. What became known as the Second Hundred Days was soon underway.

THE SECOND HUNDRED DAYS

One of the most obvious results of the legislation in the Second Hundred Days was the high-profile Works Progress Administration, headed by Harry Hopkins (1890–1946), which was to spend $11 billion and involve itself in nearly one and a half million projects, from the building of schools and airfields to the Federal Art Project, in the years between 1935 and its eventual dismantling in 1943.

Another far-reaching and innovative piece of legislation in the Second Hundred Days was the National Labor Relations Act, known as the Wagner Act after the name of its principal sponsor in Congress. Under the NRA there had been a National Labor Relations Board, but it had been a relatively powerless institution, shackled both by the terms under which it had been established and by the administration's then unwillingness to stand firm against giant corporations that ignored its regulations.

In February 1935 Senator Robert F. Wagner (1877–1953) introduced his bill, unsupported by the president, proposing to make the National Labor Relations Board a permanent independent agency with widely increased powers. The bill would effectively introduce federal protection for workers joining unions. It was intended to encourage collective bargaining between management and unions as the way forward in industrial relations.

Management was less likely than labor to see this as the future, and a massive propaganda campaign against the bill was launched, largely sponsored by the National Association of Manufacturers. On radio and in newspapers, in ads and billboard posters, the message was that Wagner's bill would be dangerous, unconstitutional, and economically disastrous. The propaganda counted for nothing, however, when Roosevelt,

A cartoon mocking newspaper tycoon William Randolph Hearst, who became a ferocious opponent of FDR and the New Deal.

angered by the Supreme Court's demolition of the NRA, gave the bill his seal of approval.

The Schechter judgment by the Supreme Court was handed down on May 27, 1935. On June 4 the president sent a memo to congressional leaders in which he referred to the Wagner bill as an essential piece of legislative business. On June 27 the bill cleared its final hurdle in Congress, and Roosevelt signed the act into law eight days later. The controversial Sections 7 and 8 guaranteed that employees could join labor unions and bargain collectively through labor representatives. It compelled employers to recognize a union if more than 50 percent of the employees joined it. Employers continued to campaign against the Wagner Act, but a ruling from the Supreme Court on April 12, 1937, upheld its constitutionality.

Putting Morgan on the Spot

J. P. Morgan, Jr., and his son Junius at the Senate Building after appearing before the committee investigating Wall Street on June 2, 1933.

bing of the Senate Committee's counsel, Ferdinand Pecora, the Wall Street magnates' feet of clay continued to emerge in the spring of 1933. Pecora even summoned the legendary figure of J. P. Morgan, Jr., (1867–1943) to answer questions. Morgan was outraged, telling a friend that "Pecora has the manner and the manners of a prosecuting attorney who is trying to convict a horse thief." Yet Pecora had some pertinent questions to ask. Why, he wanted to know, had Morgan paid no income tax in 1930, 1931, or 1932. Morgan did not know—he left that to his accountants. The impression of arrogance coupled with evasiveness was only too obvious.

One of Morgan's partners, when asked to justify having a list of preferred clients to whom stock was offered below market price, replied, "They take a risk of profit; they take a risk of loss." Pecora could see little "risk of loss" in such blatant insider dealing.

The passage through Congress of the bill creating the Securities Act in May 1933 coincided with, and was helped by, a series of public revelations of corruption on Wall Street. Suddenly the public searchlight was on those bankers and financiers previously revered as giants of commerce.

A Senate investigation into Wall Street had actually been set up by the Hoover administration in 1932. It revealed that many of the most respected names on Wall Street rigged prices, lined their own pockets with large bonuses, and were happy to sell out their own customers if it would cover their own backs. Through the relentless investigation and pro-

Senate Banking and Currency Committee counsel Ferdinand Pecora, who infuriated tycoon J. P. Morgan with his pointed questions.

Easy Solutions to Hard Times

Father Charles Coughlin speaking in Cleveland in 1936. He began by supporting the New Deal but came to hate FDR and all his works.

For all the attacks of right-wing business critics, Roosevelt's most potent opposition in his first term was provided by three populists with a direct appeal to many Americans.

Huey Long was a supporter of the New Deal in 1933, but the announcement of his Share Our Wealth Society in a national radio broadcast in February 1934 was a direct challenge to Roosevelt (see Chapter 3, "Huey Long"). Long argued that the root cause of the Depression was the unequal distribution of wealth. He proposed redistributive tax measures to adjust the nation's wealth in favor of its poorest citizens. Long declared his candidacy for the presidency in August 1935 but was gunned down by an assassin the next month.

Two of the most surprising political figures thrown up by the 1930s, both of whom reached massive popular audiences, were Father Charles Coughlin (1891–1979) and Dr. Francis Townsend (1867–1960; see Volume 5, Chapter 3, "Society in the 1930s").

The Canadian-born Coughlin was a radio priest who had, like Long, originally supported the New Deal. From November 1934 his weekly broadcasts began to attack Roosevelt's administration as insufficiently committed to social justice. He established a National Union for Social Justice, which he said would work toward forcing the government to introduce "an annual wage system that is just and equitable and thus permit American workmen to preserve the American standard of living." Coughlin was always vague in identifying his enemies (which included, as well as Roosevelt, international bankers, communists, labor unions, and others) and in outlining his solutions to the nation's problems. Yet, by the first months of 1935 as many as 30 million Americans were listening to Coughlin's broadcasts. As the 1930s went on, Coughlin's broadcasts became increasingly anti-Semitic. His hatred of FDR grew stronger, and like many of the president's right-wing opponents, he began to accuse him of communist conspiracy. Coughlin also began to express sympathy with the fascist dictatorships in Europe, and his obvious extremism began to lose him the support of his listeners.

The third of the populist challengers whom Roosevelt had to confront was Dr. Francis Townsend. Townsend was a retired physician whose own experience of lack of financial security led him to a scheme that he believed would set the country on the road to recovery. He suggested a $200 a month pension for all people over 60, provided they agreed to retire completely from employment and to spend the $200 dollars within one month in the United States. This would, Townsend claimed, create jobs and provide a stimulus to the economy. Townsend Clubs sprang up all over the country, and his petitions were signed by millions. Critics pointed out that the most it could do was redistribute purchasing power, and that the expense involved was hugely disproportionate to any benefits.

Alfred P. Sloan, president of General Motors and one of many rich leaders of industry who joined the anti-FDR American Liberty League.

The Social Security Act

In August 1935 another act that would have long-term consequences, the Social Security Act, became law. It enshrined certain principles of social welfare and government responsibility for its citizens that had not been recognized in the United States before. A cooperative federal–state system of unemployment compensation was established by levying a federal tax on total payrolls of those companies employing eight people or more. A tax, divided between employer and employee, was instituted to fund old-age pensions for those retiring from January 1942 onward, and the federal government agreed to share with the states the costs of those pensions already in operation. Grants were provided for financial aid for the blind, the disabled, and the homeless and for child-care services.

At the same time as the Wagner and Social Security bills were passing through Congress, Roosevelt moved further away from the advocates of business-government cooperation still in his inner circle. He announced a program of redistributive tax measures. Increased inheritance tax, gift taxes, new taxes on very large incomes, and a corporation income tax were all originally proposed. On its way through Congress the inheritance tax was removed from the proposals, and the corporation income levy was reduced in its effectiveness, but the Wealth Tax Act became law when Roosevelt put his name to it on August 31, 1935.

The tax measures of 1935 unleashed more venom against Roosevelt than almost any other act of his administration. The rich, seeing a threat to their pockets, turned on him as a traitor to his class. Some could not bring themselves to speak his name and referred only to "that man in the White House." The most powerful newspaper magnate in the country, William Randolph Hearst, had, in the heady atmosphere of the First Hundred Days, been a supporter of the New Deal. Now, on June 19, 1935, he wired a message to the editors of his papers. "President's taxation program is essentially Communism," it read. From now on Hearst's newspapers hammered home the message that the New Deal was the "Raw Deal" and that the tax plans were nothing more than a vindictive scheme to "soak the successful."

Financial contributions to the American Liberty League, perhaps the most obviously class-based opposition to Roosevelt, increased (see box, below, and Chapter 1, "Left vs. Right"). But FDR was undeterred by continuing criticism from business and from groups like the Liberty League, and he committed his administration to a direct assault on the vast powers of the public utility companies. He again called on Corcoran and Cohen to draft the Public Utilities Holding Company Act. Together they produced a bill that threatened the very existence of the giant utility companies. Their first draft included what became known as the "death sentence" clause. It proposed giving the Securities and Exchange Commission the power, after January 1, 1940, to break up any holding company that was not, in Roosevelt's words, "absolutely necessary to the continued functioning of a geographically integrated operating utility system."

The power companies responded to the bill with a campaign

American Liberty League

The Liberty League was founded in August 1934, and its members included disgruntled grandees of the Democratic Party, like the former presidential candidate Al Smith, as well as giants of business like Alfred P. Sloan of General Motors. Committed, in its own words, to "defend and uphold the Constitution" and to "foster the right to work, earn, save, and acquire property," the League claimed to be nonpartisan. In reality it was anti-FDR and anti-New Deal. Its speakers and publications put out relentless propaganda against the Roosevelt administration. The League fell into silence following FDR's triumphant reelection in 1936 and disbanded in 1940.

of fierce lobbying in Washington. Opposition to the power policy was led by Wendell Willkie, chairman of Commonwealth and Southern, who had earlier opposed the creation of the Tennessee Valley Authority and was to be Roosevelt's Republican opponent in the 1940 presidential election. Willkie accused the administration of wanting to "nationalize the power business in this country."

Concerted Resistance

The power companies paid for organized protests, by letter and by telegram, to be sent to members of Congress. Hundreds of thousands of letters and telegrams were sent. (Some were later found by a Senate investigating committee to be forgeries, and there were also implications of bribery of certain congressmen.)

In June 1935 the Senate passed the bill with the death sentence intact. However, it did so only by one vote, and the following month the House rejected the bill with the death sentence by 216–146, with many Democrats breaking party allegiance to oppose it. The rest of the bill was passed with a large majority. A further attempt early in August to push the bill through the House with the death sentence still in place also failed, and Roosevelt was obliged to compromise. Holding companies that were judged to be in charge of well-integrated power systems were exempted, and the deadline for compliance was extended two years to 1942.

It was still a stringent measure, and as one newspaper reported at the time, it "substituted only a chance for life imprisonment in the place of capital punishment." The

Public Utilities Holding Company Act represented a major triumph for those in the Roosevelt inner circle, like Frankfurter, Corcoran, and Cohen, who, drawing on the ideas of the elderly Supreme Court Justice Louis Brandeis, distrusted big conglomerates and their power. Brandeis himself had earlier written to a friend that "If F.D. carries through the Holding Company bill, we shall have achieved considerable toward curbing Bigness." Now that considerable had been achieved.

The last of the major pieces of legislation passed during the Second Hundred Days was the Banking Act, which became law on August 23, 1935. Roosevelt and the administration had little to do with the drafting and initial sponsorship of the original bill. The impetus came from the Utah banker Marriner Eccles (1890–1977), whom Roosevelt had appointed governor of the Federal Reserve Board in November 1934. Eccles was an unorthodox figure for a banker and held strong views about the need to revise the Federal Reserve System. He wanted to lessen the influence of private bankers and give ultimate control of the system to the government so that there could be some centrally directed regulation of the monetary mechanism.

In February 1935 Eccles introduced his banking bill, which passed swiftly through the House before stalling in the Senate because of the determined opposition of the Virginia senator Carter Glass. Eccles's proposals also, unsurprisingly, aroused the wrath of the private bankers, who

Wendell Willkie, who led the opposition to plans for breaking up utility companies and was FDR's Republican opponent in 1940.

joined forces with Glass to hold up the bill. Only when Roosevelt, at the beginning of the Second Hundred Days, abruptly decided that it was essential that the Eccles bill be enacted, was progress made. When it was finally passed, it included many amendments made

seven members of a newly named Board of Governors of the Federal Reserve System for 14-year terms. The members of the board, in turn, had much wider authority over the operations of the state and regional banks. The 1935 Banking Act ended by being a major part of

Smiling rivals: The president beams up at Republican nominee Alf Landon prior to the 1936 election. FDR won in a landslide.

by Glass, but still represented a significant move toward federal control of the banking system.

Glass believed he had emasculated Eccles's original radicalism, but one contemporary described the final act as a victory for Eccles "dressed up as a defeat." The president could now appoint the

the Roosevelt administration's drive to establish government control over currency and credit.

Preparing for the Election

The New Deal was renewed by the Second Hundred Days and survived those that had criticized it throughout 1934 and the first half of 1935. By the time of the presidential campaign of 1936 Roosevelt had changed his views on big business (see Volume 2, Chapter 6, "The Election of

1936"). And most businessmen, many of whom had been his supporters in 1932, had a very firm and unflattering opinion of the president. On June 27 he formally accepted the Democratic nomination before a live audience of 100,000 at Philadelphia and a radio audience of millions. In his speech Roosevelt made clear that he was no longer intent on winning over his opponents in the business and finance worlds.

•

"What they really complain of is that we seek to take away their power."

•

Comparing them to the royalists of 1776, he said, "These economic royalists complain that we seek to overthrow the institutions of America. What they really complain of is that we seek to take away their power." He went on to describe the financial world as he saw it before the legislation of his administration. "Private enterprise, indeed, became too private. It became privileged enterprise, not free enterprise." The "economic royalists" were indeed complaining that Roosevelt was seeking to overthrow the institutions of America. Most of the business world was arrayed solidly against him.

THE REPUBLICAN CHALLENGE

To challenge Roosevelt the Republicans chose the only member of the GOP who had won a state governorship in 1934, Alf Landon of Kansas. Republican attacks on Roosevelt covered what was be-

Ex-heavyweight champion Jack Dempsey campaigns for FDR's reelection outside his restaurant in New York City in 1936.

coming familiar territory. The New Deal was condemned as undemocratic and unconstitutional, the president was accused of harboring dictatorial ambitions, and his administration's spending was claimed to be reckless and "deficit." With more bluntness than wit, Republican speakers and newspapers began to refer to Franklin "Deficit" Roosevelt. Other campaign slogans included "Let's Get Another Deal," "Defeat the New Deal and Its Reckless Spending," and, ironically in view of the outcome, "Make It a Landon-slide." More than 80 percent of the nation's newspapers endorsed the Republican challenger.

Certainly the Hearst papers were resolutely anti-Roosevelt. The Liberty League continued its attacks on the president, and conservative Democrats like Al Smith were vitriolic in their accusations. At a Liberty League banquet in Washington in January

FDR's Host of Enemies

The president's campaign manager, Jim Farley, summed up the varied opposition to FDR in a memoir published soon after the 1936 election. "The bankers were against him because they disliked his bank reform program; the financial interests…were almost frenzied in their opposition; the manufacturing and commercial interests were strongly opposed to him; and…the big metropolitan newspapers were almost a unit in the fight to bring about his overthrow."

1936 Smith claimed that the administration was pursuing socialist policies and betraying the history of the Democrats. "It is all right with me," he said, "if they want to

disguise themselves as Norman Thomas or Karl Marx or Lenin, but what I won't stand for is allowing them to march under the banner of Jefferson, Jackson, and Cleveland." More and more this was the favored tactic—to portray Roosevelt and the New Deal as antidemocratic or socialist or even communist.

Landon's campaign managers were unwilling to accept too ringing an endorsement from the Liberty League because it was so obviously a pressure group for the extremely wealthy, but the rhetoric used by Republicans was much the same as Smith's. "American voters must choose," Republican Party chairman Melvin Eaton told a rally early in the campaign, "between having their country faced with the prospect of becoming a socialized state or preserved within the terms of the Constitution."

In New York there was thinly disguised anti-Semitism in the focus put on three of Roosevelt's presidential electors—Max Zaritsky, David Dubinsky, and Sidney Hillman, who had left Russia after the abortive 1905 revolution. "The New Deal needs, wants, and cherishes the Communist vote represented by these well-known un-American agitators," one Republican advertisement read. More starkly still, another asked the rhetorical and emotive question, "Do you want another Russia?"

By now Roosevelt positively welcomed the opposition of what he called "organized money." In a speech at Madison Square Garden during the last few days of the campaign he spoke out against his attackers. "They are unanimous in their hatred of me," he said, "and I welcome their hatred." He knew that the anti-Roosevelt campaign, despite all the money and power behind it, had failed to convince the voters. On November 4 those voters duly elected him for a second term. It was another huge landslide. Roosevelt received nearly 28 million popular votes, 11 million more than Landon. In the Electoral College the tally was 523–8 in his favor. Democrats carried more than two-thirds of both Houses of Congress.

3. SECOND TERM CONFLICTS

During his first term Roosevelt had faced enormous criticism from business leaders, from the Republicans, and from mavericks like Huey Long and Father Coughlin (see box, page 72). He had gone from the consensus politics of his first few weeks in office to a bitter and often personally wounding campaign for a second term. However, the most serious challenges to the actual operation of the New Deal had come not from any of these sources but from the Supreme Court, which had struck down the NRA and, in another judgment in 1936, declared a key provision of the Agricultural Adjustment Act—relating to taxation and restrictions on production—unconstitutional. In his second term Roosevelt and his inner circle now determined to halt a continued threat to the New Deal and introduced the Judiciary Reorganization Bill in February 1937. It proposed changes in the judiciary at all levels of the federal courts, but it was its intentions for the Supreme Court that caused the most controversy. Justices of the Supreme Court, the bill proposed, could retire at the age of 70. If a Supreme Court Justice did not

Supreme Court Justice Willis Van Devanter and his family at the White House in 1932. A consistent foe of FDR, he retired in 1937.

retire at 70, the president could add an additional judge up to the number of six.

A bitter debate ensued in which Roosevelt was accused of wanting to "pack" the court, and the bill reached an impasse in Congress, with many Democrats deeply unhappy about the proposals. Roosevelt was determined to push through the Judiciary Reorganization Bill, but several events made it seem a less urgent issue than it had originally appeared. Most notably Justice Willis Van Devanter, who had been one of the most persistent Supreme Court thorns in the side of the Roosevelt administration, retired in May 1937, and he was replaced by a New Deal supporter, Senator

Hugo Black. Several New Deal Acts from the Second Hundred Days, including the Social Security Act and the National Labor Relations Act, were upheld by the Supreme Court.

Perhaps the most serious damage to the president caused by the Supreme Court dispute was the division it caused within the Democratic Party. From mid-1937 there were a significant number of Democratic congressmen who withdrew their support for the administration on several issues. That, combined with the recession of 1937 to 1938, which threatened to plunge the economy back into the darkest days of the Depression, took much of the remaining shine off the New Deal.

END OF THE NEW DEAL

In the 1938 midterm elections this division in Democratic ranks was one of the contributing factors to the gains that the Republicans made in seats in Congress for the first time since 1928. Now Republicans and conservative Democrats increasingly worked together in Congress to slow or halt New Deal legislation.

In this final phase of the New Deal only a handful of acts passed that challenged business and industry to put their house in order. In comparison with the great legislative drives of the First and Second Hundred Days, the Fair Labor Standards (Wages and Hours) Act, enacted on June 25, 1938, seemed a small step forward. In fact, by forcing businesses engaged in interstate commerce to pay a minimum wage (initially 40 cents an hour) and observe maximum working hours (initially 44 hours without overtime), it was a highly significant piece of social legislation.

Roosevelt's drive to regulate big business and to break down the power of the vast corporations did continue through early 1938. Liberals in the administration, like Secretary of the Interior Harold Ickes and the two presidential aides Corcoran and Cohen, were pressing the case that the recession owed much to the power of the trusts and monopolies. Roosevelt presented Congress with a request to authorize "a thorough study of the concentration of economic power in American industry." The establishment of the Temporary National Economic Committee was swiftly approved by Congress in June 1938.

The chairman of the committee was Senator Joseph O'Mahoney of Wyoming who was in search of, as he said, "a formula which will set business free from regimentation both by monopoly and by government." In his wish to find some midway ground that would not be seen as either anti-business or in favor of more government bureaucracy, O'Mahoney was more cautious than many New Dealers wanted. They expected more from the committee. O'Mahoney came to admit that "we have not been making the headlines because we have been altogether too dull, sedate, and conservative."

The committee enquiry ran for almost three years, producing a total of 43 reports on the workings of business. It certainly fulfilled its brief to gather information about industry. However, the long-term effects of the committee were negligible, and, as effective antitrust action, Roosevelt's appointment of Thurman Arnold (1891–1969) as assistant attorney general

•

"We have been altogether too dull, sedate, and conservative."

•

in charge of the Antitrust Division proved more significant.

Arnold, a professor at Yale Law School, was appointed in March 1938. Before the effects of World War II changed the face of American industry, he initiated more antitrust suits than any of his predecessors had. Arnold dramatically increased the number of lawyers on his staff working on antitrust cases, and they were encouraged to target excessively restrictive patents and monopolistic practices of companies from

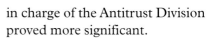

Thurman Arnold being sworn in as assistant attorney general in the Antitrust Division in March 1938. He proved an effective prosecutor.

industrial giants like General Electric to smaller firms such as housing contractors.

By the latter half of 1938, however, the New Deal had effectively run its ideological course. Congress had grown increasingly conservative, and more and more Democrats were less and less enthusiastic about radical ideas and their implementation. Roosevelt had himself moved from his position in 1933, where he had wanted to involve business in a partnership with government, through a period in which he had recognized the need to impose regulation on those big companies and financial institutions that were unwilling to accept such cooperation except on their own terms, to what by 1938 had become a kind of stalemate.

The Focus Shifts

The continued failure of the economy to respond dramatically to government action—there were still nine million unemployed nearly 10 years after the Wall Street Crash—reduced confidence in the New Deal even among its supporters. In any case, Roosevelt was more and more focused on events in Europe and in Asia (see Volume 6, Chapter 4, "The Road to War"). The New Deal and FDR's long-running battle with the forces of monopoly and big business were soon to be overtaken by battles of a quite different kind and on a larger scale. By an irony of history, involvement in an unprecedentedly destructive global conflict would swiftly haul the United States and its economy clear of any vestiges of the Great Depression.

A daily scene in the 1930s outside an unemployment office in Memphis, Tennessee. The New Deal helped but did not end such plight.

SEE ALSO

◆ Volume 2, Chapter 5, **Putting People to Work**

◆ Volume 4, Chapter 1, **Left vs. Right**

◆ Volume 4, Chapter 6, **The Unionization of Labor**

◆ Volume 5, Chapter 1, **Government, Industry, and Economic Policy**

◆ Volume 6, Chapter 6, **The Legacy of the New Deal**

5

WELFARE

The Roosevelt administration introduced a range of revolutionary welfare programs to ease the hardships suffered by millions of Americans. Among them were work projects, home loans, and a social security plan.

New Yorkers wait for a free meal in 1932. Bread lines like this were a common sight all across the United States during the Depression years.

In his Second Inaugural Address, in January 1937, President Franklin D. Roosevelt declared, "Here is the challenge to our democracy: In this nation I see tens of millions... denied the greater part of what the very lowest standards of today call the necessities of life." During the Depression era government tried to meet that challenge through the provision of welfare.

1. BACKGROUND TO WELFARE

The Great Depression was the period of most extreme need the United States had ever faced. The little income working people had was spent as soon as it was earned. A third of the nation lived in substandard housing and lacked sufficient food, clothing, and medical care. The New Deal programs (see Volume 2, Chapter 2, "The Hundred Days") were set up to provide these basic necessities for all Americans.

There was no simple solution to the United States' varied problems. They were so closely intertwined and affected by so many factors—race, gender, religion,

Registration for unemployment compensation in San Francisco, California. Almost 10 million Americans were jobless in 1938, when this photograph was taken.

environment, education, health, employment—that trying wholly to eliminate them, and the poverty they caused, was futile. But in the era between the Great Crash and World War II Roosevelt, other politicians, and reformers made great strides toward this goal. The expansion of federal welfare was a major part of their work.

REASONS FOR POVERTY

Americans were poor for a wide variety of reasons. Some—the elderly, physically or mentally ill, disabled, and children—were unemployable. Their situation was made worse by the fact that they were often unable to care for or speak for themselves. Other poor people belonged to disadvantaged minority groups, which included women. Poverty was also common among those in unstable or low-paying jobs, such as migrant laborers. Finally, people who lived in areas where the economy was failing, or who worked in trades badly affected by economic downturn, often sank into poverty.

These problems had always existed but were not well documented until the Great Depression, when accurate statistical studies were made. Even then, government officials were slow to organize an accurate census of America's poor.

ATTITUDES TO THE POOR

The task of lifting the poor out of their poverty was made harder by the attitudes of other people. There was a long-held and common belief, the roots of which lay in the value Americans tradition-ally placed on self-reliance, that anyone who needed aid was lazy or morally flawed. Many middle-class Americans believed, in effect, that the poor chose to live in poverty. Hard work, they claimed, would bring the poor's problems to an end. Such myths persisted into the 20th century and continued even after the Depression years.

In fact, the poor who did have jobs often worked extremely hard. They were no different from other Americans in wanting more for themselves and their children. Before the Great Depression, however, they, like their critics, did not generally believe that they had a right to support from private charities or the federal govern-ment. They struggled to survive, and if at all possible to improve their lives, on their own.

WHAT IS WELFARE?

The changes introduced by the New Deal and successive reforms challenged Americans' traditional view of welfare. The terminology used to discuss welfare was an important indication of attitudes

In this New York City scene from 1930 police distribute bread and eggs to the unemployed. This was the first food handout provided in the city during the Depression.

Welfare Today

Welfare today falls into two main types. Public assistance, or means-tested relief, is provided to people who need help for a specific reason and do not have means to provide for themselves. Aid to Families with Dependent Children is an example. The second type, social insurance, meets a specific purpose, such as old age or disability, but is paid to everyone who qualifies, whatever their means. Examples are Social Security and unemployment insurance.

toward the subject. In the Depression era the term "welfare" was rarely employed. "Relief" was the favored term, since it distinguished this form of aid, which was earned, from "charity," for which no work was demanded in return. People brought up to respect self-reliance were reluctant to take help for which they had not in some way labored.

PRE-DEPRESSION WELFARE

Before the Great Depression the U.S. welfare system was mainly based on private endeavors, many of which were organized by churches. Public programs were limited. Although some city and county agencies offered limited relief programs for the poor, they were an entirely local responsibility: State governments paid them little or no reimbursement. People who fell on hard times were often taken in by relatives. Those without families went to city- or county-run poorhouses or work farms.

The Reformers

The movement toward increased public welfare provision began in the late 19th century. Advocates for the poor, called reformers, included journalists and a new breed of professional social worker. Such workers trained at specialized schools and made studies of poor people's lives. Some moved into "settlement houses," that is, homes in city slums. They aimed to experience how the poor lived and to help them. The first settlement house, Hull House, Chicago, was founded by Jane Addams in 1889.

Reformers believed the causes of poverty were not immorality and laziness, but economics and the grim environments in which many were forced to live. They aimed to make government aware of these problems and to inform ordinary people through books and newspaper articles. For example, in his book *How the Other Half Lives* (1890) journalist and photographer Jacob Riis exposed the misery of life in New York City's immigrant slums.

The reformers suggested many ways to improve the lives of the poor. They included birth control to limit population growth, the elimination of substandard housing, and the transformation of inner-city environments, for example, by building playgrounds. Reformers also sought better conditions in poorhouses and the abolition of child labor. Community Chest funds were set up to pay for these ambitious welfare plans.

2. GOVERNMENT INTERVENTION

The first government-sponsored welfare service, for widowed women with young children, was introduced in the early 1900s. Despite the obvious need—any

Children's Welfare

In the United States government welfare provision for children began in 1912, when the U.S. Children's Bureau was established as part of the Labor Bureau. Its role was to protect children, and especially child workers. But in the Depression years the bureau could not even begin to meet the welfare needs of America's young people.

•

"You stole, you cheated through.... Stole clothes off lines, stole milk off back porches, you stole bread."

•

Children endured hardship for many reasons. Poverty and unemployment led to family breakdown. Many parents placed their sons and daughters in orphanages. Others placed children there because they were too costly to feed and clothe. By 1932, 20,000 children lived in orphanages simply because their parents had no money.

When parents lost their homes through failure to make rent or mortgage payments, children were sometimes left to fend for themselves. Experts estimate some 900,000 Americans under the age of 18 spent the Depression years wandering from place to place as tramps. Many were killed as they tried to jump on railroad trains for free rides. One 15-year-old hobo recalled how such children survived, "You stole, you cheated through. You were getting by, survival. Stole clothes off lines, stole milk off back porches, you stole bread."

The incidence of child labor rose sharply during the Depression. Many parents were dependent on what their children could earn for small tasks such as shining shoes or for factory work. But moves to ban the practice gradually increased. The cotton industry ended child labor as part of its NIRA code. The 1938 Fair Labor Standards Act banned interstate commerce in goods made by under-16s, dealing child labor a fatal blow.

Education was seriously disrupted by the Great Depression. Across the nation thousands of teachers were laid off because there was no money to pay them. In some states, such as West Virginia, many schools closed. Another effect of economic hardship was that many children who would once have stayed on at school left as soon as they could to earn money. The National Youth Administration (NYA), set up by the federal government in 1935, gave many high-school students grants and part-time jobs so they could afford to stay in education. Some one and a half million of them benefited from this scheme, which also helped college students in financial need.

This 1939 photograph shows children of migrant laborers living in a Florida shack. Migrants were among the poorest people in Depression-era America, so their children suffered particularly high deprivation levels.

work women found was usually low-paid and childcare often unavailable—the stigma attached to accepting a handout remained. In addition, women generally had to prove their "moral fitness" before aid was granted to them. Few were judged suitable for help.

As the 20th century went on, more public welfare initiatives were slowly introduced. They included the establishment of the U.S. Children's Bureau in 1912 (see box, page 83). It was not until the advent of the Depression, however, that the government began to take responsibility for its citizens in earnest.

WELFARE UNDER HOOVER

President Herbert Hoover (1874–1964) expressed his desire to, "with the help of God, be in sight of the day when poverty shall be banished in the nation." Hoover believed, however, that federal relief was wrong. Although he was widely criticized for this opinion, both at the time and by later historians, Hoover was reflecting

the views of many. During his presidency, from 1929 to 1933, he called on community agencies and private charities to solve the United States' problems (see Volume 1, Chapter 7, "Hoover: The Search for a Solution").

Finally the economic crisis forced Hoover to sanction federal intervention. Social conditions had become desperate. Demonstrations, rent strikes, and looting were common. The poor scrounged or survived on private charity. It was often provided by civic or church groups, such as the American Red Cross, the Women's Christian Temperance Union, the United Fund, the Salvation Army, and local Elks' lodges. Organized crime played its part, too. Gangster Al Capone is rumored to have run a soup kitchen on Chicago's South Side.

In January 1932 Hoover's administration established the Reconstruction Finance Cor-

The sandwich board worn by this young woman advertises the Emergency Unemployment Relief Appeal. It was launched in 1932 to help New York's jobless.

poration (RFC). Led by Texan Jesse H. Jones (1874–1956), the RFC loaned government money—$1.78 billion in the first year alone—to save banks and other businesses from collapse. It went on to fund schemes from irrigation and housing to setting up American Airlines. In July Congress passed the Emergency Relief and Construction Act. It provided for the distribution of $300 million of relief funds among the states.

3. THE NEW DEAL

Efforts to set up a comprehensive relief program started with the election of Franklin D. Roosevelt. Federal government set out to provide poor Americans with food, shelter, and health care. In

Unwelcome Welfare

Dorothy Day, a Catholic journalist, recalled her opposition—common at the time—to state welfare: "The whole program of unemployment, Social Security, was a confession of the failure of our whole social order. And confession of failure of Christian principles: that man, in fact, did not look after his brother. That he had to go to the State...."

addition, it aimed to provide unemployment insurance, and eventually work, for people who had lost their jobs and Social Security for senior citizens (see box, page 96). Some of the programs introduced by the New Deal still exist today.

Eleanor Roosevelt summed up the fundamental change in attitude that had taken place since the turn of the century: "In the nineteenth century...there was no recognition that the government owed an individual certain things as a right. Now it is accepted that the government has an obligation to guard the rights of an individual so...that he never reaches a point at which he needs charity."

Many Americans opposed the creation of a welfare state, that is, a state in which government plays a large part in supporting its citizens during time of need. Some saw it as a step on the road to socialism or communism, suspicion of which had been high since the Red Scares of the early 1920s. Roosevelt himself expressed a wariness of the detrimental effects of welfare. He declared: "Continued dependence upon relief induces a spiritual and moral disintegration...destructive to the national fiber." To guard against this, Roosevelt repeatedly made it clear that government assistance was intended to provide only temporary help. He did not intend a permanent alteration of the American system.

EMPLOYMENT PROGRAMS

Several factors, including foreign immigration and steady migration from rural areas to urban centers,

Unemployed men march through Camden, New Jersey, in 1935. They belonged to the Unemployed Union, one of many self-help groups set up in the Depression.

led to a shortage of jobs for Americans. By 1933 about 15 percent of the total U.S. population, more than 18 million Americans, were dependent on relief.

Among the first urgent tasks for Roosevelt's administration was to get able-bodied Americans back

•

"...dependence on relief induces a spiritual and moral disintegration."

•

to work. To this end the federal government instituted a variety of work programs across the country that employed people in many trades and professions (see Volume 2, Chapter 5, "Putting People Back to Work"). The programs allowed men to work in exchange for pay

and so to avoid the stigma of accepting direct, unearned relief.

The first relief program was the Federal Emergency Relief Administration (FERA), established in April 1933, which was replaced by the Works Progress Administration in 1935. The program began with $500 million for direct aid. It was administered by Harry Hopkins (1890–1946), a former social worker and friend of the president. He distributed the money as cash relief and as payment for work on government-subsidized employment programs.

Later that same year the Civil Works Administration (CWA) was formed. Also led by Hopkins, it existed only in the winter of 1933 to 1934, when it employed about four million people. In return for road-building, street repair, and similar projects they received about $15 per week, more than the benefits available through FERA.

The Civilian Conservation Corps (CCC) was also set up in 1933. Corps employees, who were

mostly young men between the ages of 18 and 25 but also included some veterans, worked on outdoor projects such as planting trees, stocking lakes and rivers, and constructing trails, shelters, and

Men working for the Rural Electrification Administration. This small federal agency helped millions of people by bringing electricity to remote areas.

campgrounds. In addition to jobs the CCC gave its workers food, medical care, and education. They also received $30 per month, of which $25 was sent directly to their families at home. Together, FERA, the CWA, and the CCC helped more than 28 million

people in total, a record number of people on public welfare.

The second New Deal, which began in 1935, brought more legislation and set up more agencies. On May 6 Congress created the Works Progress Administration to replace FERA.

Much like its predecessors, and again under the leadership of Harry Hopkins, the WPA was designed to provide jobs for the unemployed. Many were put to work on construction projects, such as bridge-, school-, or tunnel-building. Unlike earlier employment programs, the WPA also set out to help white-collar professionals—office workers, professors, teachers, and others—by finding

them employment in educational, library, health, and related community projects.

Some WPA participants had the option to join projects under the umbrella of "Federal One." This WPA arm was responsible for employing artists and other creative people in programs such as the Federal Theater Project, the Federal Art Project, the Federal Music Project, and the Federal Writers' Project (see Volume 5, Chapter 4, "The Arts in the Depression").

The WPA reached right across the United States in an effort to give all Americans an equal chance at work. However, even at its height it employed only about three million people. They earned an average of just $52 per month.

CRITICISM

There was much criticism of FERA and the WPA. Many people claimed they were both make-work programs. To illustrate their case, they pointed to the questionable public value of some of the tasks performed by the agencies, which included, for example, the construction of a tunnel between buildings at a Pennsylvania mental hospital.

The criticism was not taken lightly by those who participated in the employment programs. In May 1939 the New York City Federal Theater Project staged a satirical review called *Sing for Your Supper*. One of its sketches, "Leaning on a Shovel," addressed the claim that work projects encouraged laziness. A verse from one song in the sketch ran:

When you look at things today
Like Boulder Dam and TVA
And all those playgrounds
*   where kids can play*
We did it—by leaning on a
*   shovel!*

Other people criticized the WPA for different reasons. Some alleged that state and local agency administrators gave jobs to people who could grant them political favors, rather than to those who were best qualified or most suitable. Conservatives protested that the program smacked of socialism. Their most frequent targets were the arts programs, whose work they often declared was too left-wing or controversial. Business people complained that the program amounted to unfair competition for private industry.

MINORITY GROUPS

Accounts describing the success of the work programs often fail to mention the great numbers of people who were underserved, if served at all, by their existence. Since they were not U.S. citizens, immigrants were simply not allowed to join the programs. Although program administrators tried to prevent discrimination, African Americans and other minorities were also typically excluded. The effect of federal programs on their welfare was often negligible or nonexistent.

The virtual exclusion of minority groups from the programs was all the more pronounced because their need for assistance was particularly great. Black people, especially black men, suffered the highest unemploy-

ment rates. By 1931, 38 percent of the jobless in Pittsburgh, Pa., were black, despite the fact that blacks formed just 8 percent of the city's population. Black women, who mainly worked on farms or as domestic servants, were often forced to accept pay cuts and longer working hours. Employers knew that they would not dare to protest because there were always others waiting to take their jobs. Often the New Deal also failed to protect black civil rights (see Volume 5, Chapter 2, "Equality for Some"): Roosevelt himself refused to support an antilynching law because he was afraid of antagonizing Southern politicians.

The Tennessee Valley Authority (TVA), the leading regional planning program, provides an example of how New Deal agencies paid lip service to racial equality. Arthur E. Morgan, chairman of the TVA's three-man board of directors, insisted in 1934 that the TVA would not practice racial discrimination. He declared, on the contrary, that jobs would be given to minorities in proportion to their numbers in the local population. This did not happen. Black people found it difficult even to obtain application forms for employment on TVA projects.

The WPA and its affiliated National Youth Administration

A poster advertising the Federal Theater Project review called Sing for Your Supper, *which was performed at New York City's Adelphi Theater in 1939.*

(NYA) (see box, page 83) are generally considered to have given African Americans a fairer share of aid than other federal agencies. In 1936 the NYA had created a "Division of Negro Affairs," headed by leading advocate of African American rights Mary McLeod Bethune (1875–1955). Bethune was also head of the unofficial Federal Council on Negro Affairs, a group of 40 government agency administrators sometimes known as the Black Cabinet (see Volume 2, Chapter 6, "The Election of 1936"). Bethune worked with Eleanor Roosevelt to ensure that the NYA helped place young African Americans in worthwhile jobs. By March 1938 more than 480,000 black people between the ages of 18 and 25 were employed in a great variety of NYA projects.

Welfare and Women

It was hard for single women to find employment in the Depression since any available jobs normally went to men. Family breakdowns meant millions of married women had to raise their children alone. Eleanor Roosevelt championed the welfare of women, holding a White House Conference on their needs in 1933. Agencies such as the WPA set up women's divisions.

The Committee of the American Red Cross chapter in Mount Bayou, Mississippi. The chapter, whose members were all African Americans, helped many in need.

REORGANIZATION

The Reorganization Act of 1939 made important changes in the WPA. It was renamed the Work Projects Administration and placed under the jurisdiction of the Federal Works Agency. As a result it was no longer specially funded by Congress. The WPA's mandate changed, too, since it returned wholly to its original mission of providing jobs in public works projects. Even they were reduced, while the Federal Theater Project was eliminated altogether, and remaining "Federal One" projects had to find other funding sources.

The onset of World War II in 1939, and direct U.S. involvement in the war from 1941, meant that more private sector jobs were available to people needing work. The government finally eliminated all the WPA agencies in July 1943.

HOUSING

The housing crisis was one of the greatest challenges to face the Roosevelt administration. Inner cities were growing increasingly crowded as immigration from abroad and migration from rural areas rose. It was very hard to find decent, affordable homes. The tenements available provided only substandard accommodation. Many people had to live in shacks. To solve these problems, much new legislation was enacted. It created many housing programs overseen by a variety of agencies.

HOME LOANS

The Home Owners' Loan Corporation was a temporary agency formed in 1933. Its purpose was to stabilize the real-estate market. Residential property values had fallen greatly, and mortgage debt had soared. The corporation refinanced the loans of about a million homeowners, allowing them to repay their debt in smaller amounts over a longer term than originally agreed, and often at a lower interest rate.

A new piece of legislation, the National Housing Act, followed in

A member of the Mount Bayou Red Cross prepares food parcels for black farmers in 1930. The farmers needed aid because drought had ruined their crops.

June 1934. It laid down a variety of codes and regulations that guaranteed Americans well-built homes at prices they could afford. Among the act's provisions was the establishment of inspections to make sure new dwellings were constructed properly. The act also set up the Federal Housing Administration (FHA), an agency that insured home loans made by mortgage lenders, reduced the down payment on a new home from 30 to 10 percent of the home's value, and made it possible to repay mortgages over 30 rather than 20 years. The combined result of these initiatives was to begin an increase in urban home-ownership that continued long afterward. About 46 percent of Americans owned their homes in 1930. By 1980 that figure had risen to 65 percent. In general, home-ownership programs helped the middle classes buy housing in new suburbs, but made little impact on the plight of the poor.

PUBLIC HOUSING

During the Depression thousands of the urban poor lived in slums. The first New Deal provision to improve their housing situation came in the National Industrial Recovery Act of 1933. It allowed funding for the construction of public housing in American cities where a serious homes shortage could be proved. Some 22,000 housing units were built before the act was declared unconstitutional in 1935.

Federal action to deal with the housing crisis encouraged 31 states to pass their own housing legis-

An African American recipient of welfare. The photographer noted that this man was one of the few to protest about the indignity of the long wait in benefit lines.

lation. Meanwhile the Public Works Administration (PWA), set up in 1933, undertook a survey of substandard housing throughout the United States. Its findings prompted several interest groups to lobby Congress jointly for more good, affordable homes.

The lobbyists were led by New York senator Robert F. Wagner (1877–1953) (see box, page 91), who championed the Housing Act, also known as the Wagner-Steagall Act, of 1937. The act's preamble stated that its purpose was "to remedy the…acute shortage of decent, safe, and sanitary dwellings for families of low income…[the lack of which is] injurious to the health, safety, and morals of the citizens of the Nation."

The new legislation set up the United States Housing Authority, which was given $500 million of federal funds to distribute for the construction of housing projects. No state was to receive more than 10 percent of the money. The projects were to be run by local administrators, who had to

undertake slum clearance at the same time as building new homes. By 1940 this program had provided more than 118,000 housing units in 334 projects.

HOUSING AID FOR FARMERS

The Roosevelt administration also introduced special housing aid programs for farmers, who played a vital role in the U.S. economy. Among the earliest legislation to ease their housing problems was the Emergency Farm Mortgage Act of May 1933. Its purpose was to protect farmers unable to pay their mortgages from foreclosure (forced repayment), which often involved the seizure of their farms. The act arranged for a federal agency called the Farm Credit Administration to provide them with new mortgage loans. By December 1933 it had already handed out about $100 million.

Roosevelt's administration also set up a range of agencies to help farmers who, as a result of unwise land use, drought, or other circumstances (see Volume 3, Chapter 2,

The United States Housing Authority set out to transform this run-down area of New Orleans, Louisiana, in 1940. The result appears below right.

"Shadow over the Countryside"), were no longer able to make a living from the land. There was the Subsistence Homestead Division, which was founded as part of the Interior Department following the 1933 National Industrial Recovery Act. Its aim was to relocate people in new model communities, where they would grow food and create self-sufficient neighborhoods. Over the next two years some 7,000 people, from city slums as well as failing farms, moved into about 60 of these settlements.

In 1935 the Subsistence Homestead Division was absorbed into a new agency called the Resettlement Administration (RA). It continued to set up communities on the existing model, but also established three new-style suburban settlements, known as Greenbelt towns. They were Greenbelt, near Berwyn, Maryland, after which the towns were named, Greenhills, near Cincinnati, Ohio, and Greendale, near Milwaukee, Wisconsin. They comprised planned, affordable housing with gardens, surrounded by areas of agricultural land.

Hightstown, another special housing project, was built in New Jersey at the urging of Jewish garment workers. They aimed to support a utopian society by pooling their labor to run garment factories and agricultural cooperatives. The businesses were not successful, but the town was. It was sold by the government in 1945 and later changed its name to Roosevelt.

The RA was itself absorbed into another agency, the Farm

Security Administration (FSA), which was set up in 1937. Unlike previous rural housing programs, the FSA worked to keep smaller farmers on their land. It provided loans to the rural poor, either to

The same area of New Orleans (see above) after the Housing Authority had finished its work. Clean, bright housing, plants, trees, and a wide new road have completely altered the scene.

enlarge their holdings or, in the case of both tenant farmers and sharecroppers, to buy the land they already farmed. However, fewer than 2 percent of U.S. tenant farmers received financial help from the agency.

FSA programs were criticized by other governmental agencies, especially those that supported more powerful agricultural interests. Roosevelt also came under attack in both 1939 and 1940 from a professional farmers' organization, the American Farm Bureau Federation. This condemnation was prompted in part by frustration at the declining political influence of the farming lobby. Ultimately, however, the Federation's efforts weakened,

then ended, farming aid programs as World War II approached.

Expert assessments of New Deal assistance to farmers vary. Many historians accept that the aid programs restored income and self-respect to thousands of farmers. Others point out that their effect was smaller than might have been expected. Between them the RA and FSA had planned to relocate about 500,000 families. Only about 4,400 were in fact moved.

HEALTH CARE

During the Great Depression large numbers of Americans had to go without health care. Many of those who did seek treatment could not pay their bills. In 1932

Hightstown

C. B. Baldwin, a government worker, recalled the failure of the idealistic community: "The enthusiasm was terrific. They had a hell of a good first year, but you take people out of a highly competitive situation and try to set up a Utopian society, you're gonna have some difficulty."

the biggest concern voiced by American workers was the lack of public health insurance. The government addressed these

Robert F. Wagner

As Democrat senator for New York State from 1927, German-born Robert F. Wagner (1877–1953) drove through important welfare legislation such as the National Industrial Recovery Act of 1933 and the Social Security Act of 1935. He is associated above all with the National Labor Relations (Wagner) Act of 1935 (see Chapter 6, "Labor"). Wagner introduced and supported the act despite Roosevelt's opposition. After it was enacted, the law transformed the relationship between management and workers, whose right to collective bargaining it guaranteed. The National Labor Relations Board the act established could force managers to comply with its provisions.

Wagner was also a leading supporter of the U.S. Housing Act of 1937. Its other name, the Wagner-Steagall Act, is a reminder of his contribution to this far-reaching law.

Robert F. Wagner in 1935. Wagner was a lawyer who served on New York's Supreme Court from 1919 to 1926. He was elected senator for New York in 1927 and soon became a major political figure.

PLANNED HOUSING FIGHTS DISEASE

This Depression-era poster shows the germs that thrived in substandard housing and highlights the need for clean, new planned homes.

health care. The American Medical Association (AMA) responded in 1934 by reducing medical school admissions. By training fewer doctors, it aimed to increase demand for their services and so maintain high prices. This tactic only served to create greater problems for poor Americans.

Health Surveys

Statistics published by health agencies showed the huge disparity between medical care for the rich, who could afford doctors' fees, and the poor, who could not. The National Health Survey of 1935–1936 reported that the poorest were at greatest risk of illness but received the least medical care. In 1938 Surgeon General Thomas Parran wrote: "It is apparent that inadequate diet, poor housing, the

hazards of occupation, and the instability of the labor market… create…health problems."

RURAL HEALTH CARE

There were few physicians in rural areas. Programs such as the Frontier Nursing Service in Kentucky provided some medical care. The duties of service nurses varied. They assisted in childbirth, gave vaccinations, and educated residents about how to prevent diseases common among the poor of the region, such as an eye infection called trachoma. Patients often paid with goods like hay, pigs, or pieces of furniture.

NATIONAL HEALTH CARE?

Many Americans advocated the introduction of a comprehensive health-care program. Although politicians debated the issue, no legislation to launch such a plan was enacted. The last attempt to set up national health care was the 1939 Wagner bill. Strong AMA opposition and other factors prevented its passage.

Some of the health-care gap was filled by private health

problems by introducing a wide range of measures to provide health care for the needy.

FERA granted some funds for medical care, nursing, and also emergency dental work. Federal agricultural agencies organized prepayment plans that allowed farmers to save small, regular amounts for medical care they might need in the future. PWA building projects included sewer systems and hospitals. The Social Security Act of 1935 (see box, page 96) provided for care of disabled and dependent children. The federal government matched individual state care funds.

Among the last pieces of New Deal legislation was the Food, Drug, and Cosmetic Act of 1938. It promoted public health by banning manufacturers from making false claims about drugs and devices they produced.

Doctors grew very concerned about federal intervention in

The Social Security Act of 1935 established a child welfare plan that sent many nurses out to the homes of the poor.

insurance, provided by new companies such as Blue Cross-Blue Shield. This was the origin of the two-tier health system in the United States today. Private insurance is bought by the rich or made available by employers. Government health services are provided for the poor.

LEGISLATION

Some legislation to give federal aid to the needy was enacted under Hoover. However, it was only after Roosevelt became president in March 1933 that a wide-ranging program of social welfare laws was introduced. Already during the president's first months in office, the so-called Hundred Days, Congress passed 15 New Deal acts.

The two major areas of legislation to affect welfare in the Depression were labor law and Social Security law. Both had a huge effect on the lives of many American citizens.

Labor Law

Among the first labor laws of the Roosevelt administration was the National Industrial Recovery Act (NIRA) of 1933 (see Chapter 6, "The Unionization of Labor"). It encouraged industries to prepare new codes of practice, which had to include labor-friendly provisions. They included maximum working hours, minimum wages, and safe working conditions. The codes also gave workers the right to organize into unions, and unions the right to bargain with management on behalf of the whole labor force, a practice known as collective bargaining. By mid-1933 more than 500 American industries had codes in place.

A National Labor Relations Board was established in 1934 to enforce the collective bargaining agreements provided for in NIRA. At first, big business supported this government intervention. However, the excessive bureaucracy governing the implemen-

American Red Cross members give seeds to segregated lines of Arkansas farmers in 1930. The seeds were used to replant drought-hit fields.

tation of the codes soon led to widespread disillusion. Business leaders came to regard federal policy as an unhelpful and irrational burden designed to bring them under the rule of both government and organized labor. Finally, in May 1935 the United States Supreme Court ruled NIRA unconstitutional (see Chapter 2, "The Supreme Court").

In July 1935 Congress enacted a new labor law, the National Labor Relations Act, commonly known as the Wagner Act. Like its predecessor, it gave employees the right to organize and required employers to participate in collective bargaining discussions with unions. In addition, the Act created a new National Labor Relations Board (NLRB) to oversee collective bargaining agreements. The board continues to function today.

The constitutionality of the new act was challenged in 1937, but the Supreme Court allowed it to stand. In the same year the court made another important decision affirming that minimum wage provisions applied to women as much as men.

The 1938 Fair Labor Standards Act reinforced earlier labor laws. It limited working hours to 44 per week and established a minimum wage of 25 cents per hour. The new wage affected 12.5 million people. The act also effectively prohibited child labor (see box, page 83).

Social Security

In the Depression era Americans became increasingly aware of the need to insure themselves against poverty, particularly in old age or during periods of unemployment. As a result, some people began to campaign for the introduction of comprehensive social security.

The concept of an American social security program was first promoted by 67-year-old doctor Francis Townsend. The Townsend Old-Age Revolving Pension Plan, commonly called the Townsend Plan, was made public in 1933 (see Volume 5, Chapter 3, "Society in the 1930s"). It proposed to pay a $200 monthly pension to all men and women over 60. The payments were to be made on the understanding that recipients were not to look for employment and were to spend the funds within 30 days. A sales tax on business of a little more than 2 percent was proposed to fund the scheme. Dr. Townsend based this figure on the gross (pretax) sales receipts of U.S. businesses and industries, which he had estimated at approximately $935 billion per year.

Townsend's nonprofit Old Age Revolving Pensions, Ltd., was founded in 1934 to promote his plan. Soon after its foundation, about 500,000 people across the United States joined "Townsend Clubs" to promote the cause. Many economists thought Townsend's plan unworkable and impossibly expensive. Their views did not prevent the clubs from attracting about two million members by 1935. As the clubs' numbers grew, so did their political power. Members wrote congressional leaders and other politicians, pushing them to enact the plan. Some politicians drafted legislation that would do so, but none came close to becoming law.

The Townsend camp had several national figures among its allies. They included Louisiana senator Huey P. Long, whose "Share-Our-Wealth" movement aimed to redistribute money from rich to poor Americans (see Chapter 3, "Huey Long"). Another Townsend supporter was Roman Catholic priest Father Charles Coughlin, whose radio shows attacked capitalism and promoted a range of financial schemes (see box, page 72).

Roosevelt saw the Townsend movement as a major political threat. He was not alone. Other

> # Townsend's Plan
>
> George Murray, editor of the Townsend Movement's newspaper, recalled how Townsend's plan began: "His idea: a gross income tax of two percent on everybody in the country, no exceptions. Proceeds to be divided among all people over sixty, the blind and disabled, and mothers of dependent children. They had to spend it within thirty days. He wasn't a great economist, but he had something figured out in his mind."

This billboard was displayed in Texas in 1935. It advertises the Townsend Plan, which aimed to introduce pensions for the over-60s, but was never implemented.

In this 1938 scene workers in New Jersey sit outside homes provided by their employers. Many corporations had by that time discontinued such benefits.

politicians and cabinet members, among them Labor Secretary Frances Perkins, were disturbed by the fervor of Townsend's supporters. Edwin Witte, director of the Committee of Economic Security, called the plan "a terrific menace which is likely to engulf our entire economic system." He feared that it might result in demands for overextravagant pensions that the nation simply could not afford.

The Social Security Act of 1935 (see box, page 96) ended the push to enact the Townsend Plan. However, the Townsend Clubs remained numerous and active until late 1936, after which they gradually disbanded.

PRIVATE CHARITY

The need for public assistance programs during the Depression era was made greater by the decline of private charities. Support for charitable institutions was strong in the United States until the late 1920s. But between 1929 and 1932, as the Depression bit, about 400 private welfare agencies closed. They were unable to keep pace with the demand for services, which was rising just as donor contributions were falling.

Another private welfare system crumbled. It was welfare capitalism, in which private corporations provided their employees with benefits such as housing and medical care. The system had grown up in the 19th century and reached its peak in the 1920s. Employers thought it preferable to interference in welfare issues from unions and government. The system also found favor among many social reformers, who believed it would help curb industrial unrest.

In the Great Depression, however, welfare capitalism gradually collapsed. Thousands of employees were laid off and were no longer eligible for corporate benefits. But in any case, many corporations could not afford to continue their welfare programs. Workers therefore turned instead to the steadily growing unions, and to government, to meet their urgent welfare needs.

Some forms of private charity continued in the Depression era.

Foundations originally set up by wealthy industrialists such as steel magnates Andrew Carnegie and Henry Frick, and oil baron John D. Rockefeller, still poured money into a range of cultural programs. The Carnegie Foundation, for example, funded public libraries. But these activities did little to tackle society's basic problems.

4. ROOSEVELT'S ACHIEVEMENTS

In one of his 1934 radio talks, known as the fireside chats, Roosevelt told Americans that they might judge the success of his administration and its welfare policies by asking themselves a series of questions, such as: "Are you better off than you were last year? Are your debts less burdensome? Is your bank account more secure? Are your working conditions better? Is your faith in your own individual future more firmly grounded?" Roosevelt was sure that for many citizens, the honest answer to these questions was "Yes." Thousands agreed with him, but the President also had many forceful critics. They felt otherwise, for a variety of reasons.

ROOSEVELT'S CRITICS

Most Americans of the Great Depression era accepted that there was a moral imperative to provide for all in need. What Roosevelt's critics complained about was the way in which he fulfilled this obligation. To them the wide-ranging welfare program was unhealthy for a democratic, capitalist nation. They claimed it was steering the country toward socialism, even communism. In their view charity would have provided a better solution to the problems than did a welfare state.

Even Roosevelt did not intend to leave the legacy he did. He

The Social Security Act

The Townsend Movement forced the Roosevelt administration to consider demands for a comprehensive welfare system. Roosevelt set up a committee to study the issue in 1934, which early in 1935 sent its recommendations to Congress.

In August 1935, after much debate, the Social Security Act became law. It covered three main areas: old-age pensions, unemployment compensation, and aid for the sick and dependent children. The new pensions were funded by a 1 percent tax on employers and employees, and administered by the federal government. The payments, to people over 65, were between $10 and $85 per month, depending on the level of contributions made during working life.

Unemployment compensation was to be a federal-state plan funded by a tax on employers. Pay levels were to be fixed by individual states. Aid for the disabled and children was, by contrast, to be provided by direct grants from the federal government.

The act had serious flaws—both farm and domestic workers were excluded from its provisions, and some two-thirds of African Americans were not eligible for its benefits. But it was still a milestone in U.S. welfare law.

aimed to create a welfare system that would protect all Americans only during a time of great but temporary crisis. In fact his achievement was to establish a welfare state that has supported generations of Americans from the cradle to the grave.

"The test of our progress is not whether we add more to the abundance of those who have much; it is whether we provide enough for those who have too little." So said Roosevelt in his second Inaugural Address. The welfare programs created by his administration were not a total success, nor did they meet with universal approval. But they often served their intended function of giving vital, temporary aid to

Jobless men at an employment office. They are filing claims for the new benefits introduced by the 1935 Social Security Act and registering for available work.

Going on Relief

Ben Isaacs's clothing business failed, and eventually he realized that he had to turn to the state:

"I didn't want to go on relief. Believe me, when I was forced to go to the office of the relief, the tears were running out of my eyes. I couldn't bear myself to take money from anybody for nothing. If it wasn't for those kids—I tell you the truth—many a time it came to my mind to go commit suicide. Than go ask for relief....

"I went to the relief and they, after a lotta red tape and investigation, they gave me $45 a month. Out of that $45 we had to pay rent, we had to buy food and clothing for the children. So how long can that $45 go? I was paying $30 on the rent. I went and find another a cheaper flat, stove heat, for $15 a month. I'm telling you, today a dog wouldn't live in that type of a place. Such a dirty, filthy, dark place."

Americans. As a result, many people were able to triumph over trying economic circumstances to build new lives.

Texas farmers collect benefit checks in 1934. The idea that government should provide welfare had by then gained some acceptance.

6

THE UNIONIZATION OF LABOR

Before the Depression the vast majority of Americans who belonged to a union were skilled craftsmen. But in the 1930s there was a push to organize millions of unskilled workers. New Deal legislation favored this change, and the rise of the unions became unstoppable.

A May Day parade in 1930s New York. In many countries, May 1 is a holiday on which workers are honored.

1865–1914"). This was the era when industrialization took hold in the United States, and large numbers of people began to work in factories and mines. These individual employees had little leverage to negotiate effectively with their employers. Banding together in unions and presenting a common voice gave them more influence. The labor organizers and radicals who pioneered this development pushed incessantly for better working conditions (see box, opposite).

WELFARE CAPITALISM

From the late 19th century some firms took their own steps to improve the conditions of their employees, often in an effort to undermine the role of the labor unions. They provided for every aspect of workers' well-being, for example, by offering sports facilities, company-run "unions," pensions, and even housing. The system, known as welfare capital-

The emergence of the labor movement was a hallmark of the Depression era. For the first time, the Roosevelt administration guaranteed working-class Americans a political voice they could use to better their fortunes. Several factors coincided with the rise of the unions to increase working-class power: the poor economy, greater dependence on industrial work, pro-labor political sentiment, and the administration's insistence on giving all who wanted work the chance to earn an honest wage.

1. BACKGROUND

The groundwork for reform had been laid from the late 1800s through the 1920s (see Volume 1, Chapter 1, "The United States,

The Union Movement

The American labor movement had evolved a distinct tradition compared with unions in other industrialized countries. Evolving from the early associations formed by craftsmen such as tailors or shoemakers, the union movement that emerged in the industrial age was still based on "crafts," though they were new skills such as working with iron or acting as a railroad engineer.

The second half of the 19th century saw the emergence of the National Labor Union and its successor, the Knights of Labor, to argue not only for workers' rights but for broad political reform that would produce a fairer society. Such

organizations echoed the involvement of European unions in promoting socialist and communist political parties. In 1886, however, the American Federation of Labor (AFL) was formed by moderates to undermine the influence of the Knights of Labor. It affirmed a union tradition that focused on pay and conditions rather than socialist politics. The AFL's conservatism helped win public support for union causes, as did tragedies such as the Triangle Shirtwaist Factory fire (below).

ism, reached its peak in the 1920s and remained strong for a decade more. Employers saw it as a way to ensure worker satisfaction without union or government interference. Many politicians and others saw it as more in keeping with "American" values of individualism and paternalism than the union system.

Welfare capitalism thrived in America, with its large firms, weak unions, and government reluctance to intervene in business operations. For workers, however, company control could be excessive: In rare cases people had to work at gunpoint.

WORKING CONDITIONS

Outside those corporations that adopted welfare capitalism, the majority of the working poor endured long hours and low pay in unsafe, dirty conditions. In the late 1920s a New York dock worker, for example, earned about

$20 to $30 per week. In order to survive, he often had to work a second job and borrow from loan sharks. Child employment remained relatively common.

By the time of the Depression accounts by reformers and journalists about the inhumane conditions endured by the working poor had swung public opinion in their favor. A turning point in gaining public sympathy for change had come with the Triangle Shirtwaist Factory fire of 1911. Locked in a sweatshop in a New York city block, 146 people—mainly young,

Officials put victims of the Triangle Shirtwaist Factory fire in coffins. Later, 100,000 people attended a memorial parade for the dead.

female immigrants—died when fire broke out. Fire ladders could not reach the upper floors where they were trapped.

2. THE AFL AND THE CIO
When the Depression began in the late 1920s, union membership was flagging as a result of high unemployment. The most influential labor organization of the

The Amoskeag Company

One business that took the concept of welfare capitalism extremely seriously was the Amoskeag Company. It ran a vast complex of textile mills in Manchester, New Hampshire, where almost every facility was provided for the 17,000 workers.

The company, which was founded in the 1830s, developed its strategy gradually. The idea that all the workers in the sprawling Amoskeag compound were "children" in the care of paternal employers took hold very early. However, it was not until 1910, when a comprehensive employee welfare program was introduced, that the textile company started to influence workers' lives to an extreme degree.

In addition to company housing, people were provided with nursing care, dental care, and cooking lessons. The company-run Amoskeag Textile Club held social events, from formal dinners to children's parties. There was a baseball team, too, which played on the company field.

In return for its generosity, the firm expected, and usually received, loyalty and hard work. But strikes finally reached even this haven. In combination with economic difficulties they led Amoskeag to close in 1935.

time, the American Federation of Labor (AFL), saw its membership fall from five million to fewer than three million in a decade. Founded in 1886, the AFL was made up of craft unions whose members were almost all white, skilled tradesmen. It was skeptical about industrial unionism and refused to admit the unskilled employees of mass-production industries such as automobile-making.

The AFL had also established a tradition of being effectively non-political. Many European

Top: Rows of uniform company housing on the Amoskeag site, beside the Merrimack River.

Left: The Amoskeag mills were surrounded by an imposing brick wall. Employees made their way to work through entrances like this.

Samuel Gompers

Samuel Gompers (1850–1924) was the main founder of the AFL. He was born in London, England, but emigrated to the United States with his family in 1863. Here he worked as a cigar-maker like his father, while at the same time reading widely about socialism and other political ideas. Gompers became the first president of the AFL in 1886 and was reelected to the post every year for 38 years, except in 1895.

unions—and some smaller U.S. unions, such as the Industrial Workers of the World (IWW), which had achieved prominence in the first two decades of the 20th century—campaigned for political and social reform to improve the lot of the working classes. The AFL focused on the economic rather than political struggle. It limited union activity to the achievement of higher wages and better working conditions, not political change.

THE NEW DEAL

In the financial crisis that followed the Wall Street Crash of 1929 wages fell, and working conditions worsened as desperate employers tried to cut costs. The election of Franklin D. Roosevelt as president in 1932 seemed to promise

Two strikers make their case on the streets of New York. Strikes became a common feature of political life after the birth of the CIO in 1935.

change for many working-class Americans. The National Industrial Recovery Act (NIRA) of 1933 was the first step in the process (see Volume 2, Chapter 2, "The First Hundred Days"). It gave workers the legal right to organize, that is, to join together in unions and to bargain collectively, or negotiate with employers through their unions rather than individually. Once the act became law, unionization began on a much wider scale.

Progressive labor leaders pushed hard for the inclusion of assembly-line workers and other unskilled staff in the established unions. They met strong resistance from many hard-line unionists, who did not welcome unskilled employees. The AFL also refused to change its hostility to industrial workers. The result was friction and the gradual formation of new, more open unions.

The National Labor Relations Act

In 1935 the National Labor Relations Act, also known as the Wagner Act, became law. It stated that if most workers in a firm wanted to be represented by a union in negotiations with management, employers had to accept that decision. The act also set up the National Labor Relations Board to ensure employers complied with its provisions. These changes further encouraged the formation of new unions, especially in industries where labor had not previously been organized. During the 1930s and 1940s union membership grew from 3 million to about 14 million.

THE CIO

In 1935 the union movement made a significant step toward the unionization of unskilled workers. Working within the AFL, but

Longshoremen on the New York docks in 1906. Such workers typically received very low wages for long hours of heavy labor.

contrary to its policy, officers of eight unions formed the Committee for Industrial Organization (CIO). Its main aim was to organize unskilled workers into industry-based unions rather than traditional skill-based unions.

The committee included a number of prominent labor leaders: John Llewellyn Lewis (1880–1969), leader of the United Mine Workers of America (UMW); Sidney Hillman (1887–1946), of the Amalgamated Clothing Workers; and David Dubinsky (1892–1982), of the International Ladies' Garment Workers' Union. Lewis became the CIO's first president. In 1935 the CIO was expelled from the AFL and became a separate organization; in 1938 it adopted a new name, the Congress of Industrial Organizations.

The CIO worked tirelessly in 1936 and 1937 to unionize key

industries such as steel, rubber, and auto manufacture. It sought to gain both union recognition and collective-bargaining agreements from executives of corporations such as General Motors and U.S. Steel. It would eventually even unionize bitterly antiunion shops such as the Ford Motor Company and Bethlehem Steel. CIO success was based on two main factors: the efforts of its grass-roots activists and strong national leadership that reflected Lewis's determination to establish the organization.

The CIO had a tremendous impact. It shifted the balance of power in industry, putting employees on a far more equitable footing with management. The new unions introduced shop stewards to represent workers in negotiations, grievance procedures through which they could protest unfair treatment and dismissal, and seniority systems that gave them the chance of advancement.

The Antiunion Backlash

The success of the CIO eventually led to a backlash as conservatives and business leaders became far more organized and politicized

An African American working at a foundry in the 1930s. In that era black Americans were often given the most menial, poorly paid jobs.

(see Chapter 4, "The Right-wing Backlash"). They spread misinformation and anti-union propaganda. Unionizing efforts also suffered. Attempts to organize Southern mill workers, for example, met with solid opposition from politicians at both local and state level, as well as from employers. In the South CIO organizers faced beating and kidnapping, the Ku Klux Klan, and antiunion religious revivalists, as well as competition from the AFL. A recession between 1937 and 1938 made the problems worse still. Layoffs and declines in production reduced union ranks, particularly in the automotive, rubber, and steel industries.

AFTER THE DEPRESSION

The AFL underwent a renaissance at the end of the Depression, by which time workers had come to see it as a moderate alternative to the more radical CIO. As a result, unions such as the Teamsters, Machinists, and Carpenters allied themselves with the older organization. At the same time, the AFL relaxed its hostility to unskilled laborers. Some locals, like those of the International Brotherhood of Electrical Workers, made their membership criteria less restrictive. Unionization in the service industries, such as catering and tourism, swelled AFL ranks even more. By 1940 it had about five million members, almost twice the 2.65 million of the CIO. The two organizations merged in 1955. The joint organization, known as the AFL-CIO, still exists today.

3. MINORITIES AND WOMEN

Historically, labor unions had resisted admitting minorities. Segregation of African American

Some of the female union delegates who attended a 1916 rally in New York City to support striking sleeping-car workers.

workers was common throughout the Depression and continued well into World War II (1939–1945) (see Volume 5, Chapter 2, "Equality for Some"). Like new immigrants, black people had sometimes been unwittingly used as scab labor during strikes. This served only to increase hostility from white-dominated unions. The AFL repeatedly condemned African Americans for acting as strikebreakers.

Discriminatory Jim Crow practices were as common among unions as they were among employers. Prohibitions against foreign-born workers, African Americans, and women were

standard. Samuel Gompers (see box, page 101), head of the AFL, made some effort to prevent exclusion from unions on race grounds, but achieved no real progress. If minority employees were accepted for union membership, they had to pay higher dues than whites. African Americans were typically relegated to menial tasks, even in skilled labor unions.

The situation of minority groups became worse during the Depression. Their members were

Two young strikers at a Labor Day parade in Gastonia, North Carolina, protesting against the closure of the region's textile mills.

have children. It was, they believed, not worthwhile to expend the time and effort necessary to bring female workers into unions. This sentiment was common. One member of the Transport Workers' Union (TWU) opposed the creation of a women's auxiliary to the union, saying: "They'll sit around like a sewing circle every week and get silly notions in their heads. Let 'em stay at home and cook our dinners. That's what women are good for." He and other TWU members

the last to be hired and the first to be laid off. Since they also earned less than whites, they had few savings to use in time of need. Even relief payments made to blacks were lower than those for whites.

WORKING WOMEN

In 1933 there were some three million working women in the United States. As was the case with African American workers, they were generally relegated to semiskilled jobs within their chosen trade. They also earned very low wages. During the 1930s female store clerks in New York made about $10 per week. The unions nevertheless initially paid little attention to the problems of women in the workforce.

The AFL refused to organize women. Its leaders argued that women worked purely to earn spending money before leaving industry in order to marry and

Mexicans shell pecan nuts in San Antonio, Texas. Low-paid women in the industry staged a serious strike in 1938 (see box, right).

An agricultural union speaker addresses Mexican workers during a 1938 strike in California. Despite CIO support, the strike failed.

underestimated the support women could offer. During a 1936 sit-down strike, for example, women's auxiliary members picketed outside a plant throughout the night and fed the hungry strikers inside.

Automotive workers were assisted by Women's Emergency Brigades during many sit-down strikes. The brigades were well-

•

"Let 'em stay at home and cook our dinners. That's what women are good for."

•

organized groups that cooked for the strikers and supported them in ways such as picketing. They played a special role in a 1937 General Motors' Fisher Body Plant strike in Flint, Michigan. When tear gas was fired into one of the occupied buildings, women's

brigade members broke windows to help the strikers inside breathe.

Women also staged strikes to improve their own wages and working hours. African American women, enduring discrimination on the grounds of race and gender, had particular reason to act. They typically earned one-third to one-half less than white women.

One important strike held by women took place in Richmond, Virginia, in 1937. Most of the workers in the city's tobacco industry were African American women.

Many were stemmers—people who removed the stems from the tobacco plants—who earned between just $3 and $6 for a 55-hour week. When the women voted to strike, union organization of the industry started in earnest. Whites from other unions joined the picket lines in their support.

Mexican American women staged a particularly bitter strike in San Antonio, Texas, in 1938. They worked as pecan-shellers; paid by the pound, they typically made the derisory sum of between 50 cents and $2.50 per week. When reductions in those rates were announced, the women walked out. Many were then arrested on petty charges. After 37 days the union was recognized—even though union recognition was a legal right under the National Labor Relations Act—and a wage increase awarded.

Participation in such actions empowered women, and they began to join unions in increasing numbers. In 1938 there were about 500,000 women in unions. By

The Women's Trade Union League

The Women's Trade Union League (WTUL) was founded in 1903 in response to the AFL's failure to organize working women. The League and its leading figures, including Margaret Dreier Robins, struggled for the admittance of women to unions, for legislation to protect their rights, and for higher wages. It also organized several major strikes and played an important role in the protests that erupted after the Triangle Shirtwaist Factory fire.

A cartoonist's view of "Ill-Advised Labor" blocking Uncle Sam's route to recovery. The implication is that union power is damaging the U.S.

1940 that figure had risen to 800,000. But although the CIO did help to organize these women, their problems and their contributions were very rarely mentioned in union literature.

4. PROMINENT FIGURES

Despite the efforts of the thousands of unsung organizers who worked in the field, the labor movement was only as strong as its leaders. Outspoken, salt-of-the-earth labor advocates were attracted to the union movement throughout the 1930s and 1940s. Many followed in a U.S. tradition of passionate workers' champions that included Eugene Debs (1855–1926), founder of the American Railway Union, and William "Big Bill" Haywood (1869–1928), founder of the Industrial Workers of the World.

JOHN LLEWELLYN LEWIS

John Llewellyn Lewis was born to organize. The son of a Welsh coal miner who emigrated to the United States, Lewis did various jobs as a young man, including coal mining. In 1907 he went back to mining as an organizer and two years later became head of his union local. He ascended the union ranks to become president of the United Mine Workers of America (UMW) in 1920, at the start of an extremely volatile era for the coal industry. Over the following years Lewis formed the miners' union into a powerful bloc within the AFL.

Lewis also became involved in national politics, hoping that it would help improve the coal workers' plight. He joined the Democratic Party in 1932, then worked with Franklin D. Roosevelt and other New Dealers on labor issues. During the same period Lewis steadily rebuilt the UMW and successfully organized in traditionally nonunion areas.

Lewis had one other major aim: to unionize the thousands of unskilled workers who labored in mass-production industries such as steel- and automobile-making. This development was opposed by many in the AFL and eventually led, in 1938, to the formation of the independent CIO. Lewis served as president of the CIO and its forerunner, the Committee for Industrial Organization, from 1935 to 1940. He was at his most powerful in about 1937, after which his influence began to wane.

Lewis's fading relationship with Roosevelt played a major part in his loss of influence. He was upset by the president's continued neutrality on labor issues and concerned he would take the country into war, so he supported Republican Wendell Willkie in the 1940 presidential race. Most workers did not share Lewis's sentiments. When Roosevelt won, Lewis resigned his CIO leadership and returned to the UMW.

After leading many strikes in the 1940s, Lewis worked with management to bring peace and stability to coal mining during the next decade. But as large mine operators moved in and forced

Members of a CIO local for iron, steel, and tin workers march side by side in support of a 1937 strike in Pittsburgh, Pennsylvania.

New Unions

Hundreds of new, industry-based labor unions sprang up in the United States during the 1930s and early 1940s. Among the most influential were mass-member groups like the United Automobile Workers and the Steelworkers of America. However, the spread of unionism was not restricted to heavy industry. Instead, the labor movement began to welcome employees from a huge range of white-collar professions into active groups such as the Air Line Pilots' Association and the Newspaper Guild.

ordinary miners out, many claimed his efforts had been at the expense of these hard-working men. Lewis died in obscurity in 1969.

DAVID DUBINSKY

David Dubinsky was another notable figure among labor organizers. Born in Russia, he started working in his family's bakery in Poland at 11 and soon became involved in unionism. He took part in his first strike at age 15—the family bakery was among the strike targets. As a result of his union activities, Dubinksy was labeled a labor agitator and sent to Siberia. He spent 18 months in prison before staging an escape, then secretly made his way to Belgium. There he boarded a ship bound for the United States.

Dubinksy arrived in New York in 1911. He became a U.S. citizen in 1916, joined the Socialist Party, and began working as a cloak cutter. Soon he became involved in

union activity, this time joining the International Ladies' Garment Workers' Union local. Soon he began to assume leadership roles within the union. Finally, in 1932, he was elected its president.

Dubinksy now had the monumental task of reorganizing the union, which was in debt and split into warring factions. The differences were based in Marxist politics, but made worse by racial and

John Llewellyn Lewis, president of the UMW, is pictured second from the right during negotiations with mine owners.

religious tensions. Dubinsky revived the flagging spirits of union members by calling for a strike against nonunion dress manufacturers in Philadelphia. He actively recruited volunteers to maintain the union's high profile. Under his guidance membership rose from 40,000 in 1932 to 225,000 in 1937.

Dubinsky became involved in national politics as one of the appointed labor advisers to the federal government's National Recovery Administration (see Volume 2, Chapter 5, "Putting

People to Work"). As he tried to standardize conditions throughout the garment industry, he used strikes to coerce employers into complying with federal legislation.

The rift between the AFL and the CIO placed Dubinsky in a difficult position, since he was on good terms with the leaders of both. His union remained independent for 18 months. Then, in 1940, it was voted into the AFL.

Dubinsky remained active in the union until retiring in 1966. He worked on the boards of other public and private organizations until he died in 1982.

WALTER REUTHER

Walter Reuther (1907–1970) was born in West Virginia, the son of German immigrants. His first job was working in a Ford Motor

This damaged photograph shows David Dubinsky with Eleanor Roosevelt. Between them sits Rose Schneiderman, of the WTUL.

Company plant. Then, between 1932 and 1935, he and his brother, Victor, were employed at an automobile factory in Gorki, a city in the USSR. In 1936, after their return to the United States, the brothers founded the United Automobile Workers of America (UAW). At first companies refused to recognize it, but they were forced to do so after a series of sit-down strikes and other UAW actions.

The fact that Reuther had once lived in the USSR was often used against him. But although he had been a socialist, he later forged a reputation as a responsible labor leader dedicated to working within the U.S. political system rather than against it. After World War II his political views became even more moderate, and he denounced communist members of the CIO. In the 1948 presidential election Reuther supported the Democratic Party candidate, Harry S. Truman.

In 1952 Reuther became president of the CIO and was among those in leadership when the union merged with its former rival, the AFL, in 1955. In later years he continued to be active in union causes and the civil rights movement. Reuther died in an airplane crash in May 1970.

HARRY BRIDGES
Among the union organizers employers most feared was Harry Bridges (1900–1990), head of the West Coast International Long-shoremen's Association. Bridges was born in Melbourne, Australia, on July 28, 1900, the eldest son of Irish immigrants. His first job was working for his father as a rent collector, but this provided none of the excitement he sought. In 1920 he went to sea, bound for San Francisco.

The young Bridges soon became involved in the Australian and American sailors' unions, participating in several strikes before deciding to find a home port. He was also briefly a member of the Industrial Workers of the World, the radical union founded in 1905. The association earned him a lifelong reputation as a communist radical. In 1922 Bridges settled in San Francisco and began working on the docks as a longshoreman.

Bridges and some coworkers then joined together to form a union local, but it soon collapsed thanks to an embezzler. However, Bridges continued to be active in union organizing. He eventually came to prominence during a longshoremen's strike of May 9, 1934, which aimed to achieve union recognition, higher wages, and a 30-hour week. The action included a general strike in San Francisco that erupted into mayhem and violence (see box, opposite).

•

"That Bridge's aims are energetically radical may be admitted...."

•

Bridges' visibility during this strike established him as "the bogey man of the Pacific" in the eyes of many people. Soon afterward he was elected president of his local and in 1936 was made president of the West Coast International Longshoremen's Association. Under his direction a strike was called in October 1936 that stopped all shipping along the West Coast for a total of 98 days. The Longshoremen's Association won. In 1937 it joined the CIO.

Menacing goons approach UAW men, including Walter Reuther (third from right), in this photo, which has been marked in the past.

Many West Coast organizations expressed outrage at Bridges and his activities. Newspapers, business and civic groups, the American Legion, and the Dies Committee (later the House Committee on Un-American Activities) called for his deportation. Labor Secretary Frances Perkins reluctantly set the process in motion. In 1939 a 10-week hearing began to decide whether Bridges was a communist and so liable to be deported. In denying the deportation, the special examiner for the hearing, James M. Landis of Harvard Law School, said: "That Bridges' aims are energetically radical may be admitted, but the proof fails to establish that the methods he seeks to employ are other than those that the framework of democratic and constitutional government permits."

In 1940 another attempt was made to deport Bridges. By then the Smith Act had been passed, allowing for an alien to be deported for having once been affiliated with the Communist Party. The Senate, though skeptical about the bill's constitutionality, assigned FBI agents to investigate Bridges. The case against him was not proved, so he stayed in the United States.

Bridges had several more clashes with the federal authorities over the following years. He also fell out with the CIO, and his union was expelled from the organization in 1950. However, it remained a powerful force on the West Coast.

ROSE PESOTTA

Ukraine-born Rose Pesotta (1896–1965) was a leading member of the International Ladies' Garment Workers' Union and its only paid organizer. As such, she numbered among the highest-ranking labor organizers of the Great Depression era. Her particular achievement was to help the many thousands of women who worked in the garment industry, often earning barely $5 a week and laboring in sweatshop conditions. Pesotta's relative obscurity compared with male union organizers—both at the time and today—results largely from the fact that she was both a woman and an anarchist.

Leaders of the garment workers' union, including its president, David Dubinsky, typically sent Pesotta to organize workers in the most antiunion shops. She had great success on the West Coast in the early 1930s and was elected as a union vice-president in 1934. Pesotta refused the office on the grounds that it conflicted with her political views, but effectively served in the role for 10 years regardless. She also participated in organizing efforts with other CIO-affiliated unions like the UAW.

Throughout her union career, however, Pesotta was frequently relegated to improving morale among women and girls affected by strikes. During the 1936–1937

The General Strike

The 1934 general strike that took place in San Francisco following a call from Harry Bridges' longshoremen was a huge affair. An estimated 130,000 employees refused to work, and the city soon descended into chaos. The strikers were induced to stop their action only when 4,500 heavily armed National Guardsmen prepared to join the struggle against them. Eventually the longshoremen reached a compromise with their relieved employers.

In 1940 Roosevelt condemned the damaging feud between the AFL and the CIO. Here a New York Post *cartoonist interprets his statement.*

General Motors Fisher Body Plant strike in Flint, Michigan, she was among the union organizers beaten by thugs. Her hearing was permanently damaged as a result.

David Dubinsky mentored Pesotta, and the two agreed on many issues. They were both anti-communists with a passionate commitment to social reform. But although they had a good working relationship at first, it broke down. Pesotta was critical of Dubinsky for his sexist views. Then, in 1940 Dubinsky sent her to Los Angeles. This was, in effect, exile, since the garment industry and its related union activity were centered in New York. Pesotta also had problems with the male leader-ship in the Los Angeles union. Eventually she chose to return to work in New York City, not as a union leader but a seamstress.

During the next few years Pesotta tried to rebuild her life. This was a difficult task, especially since she sometimes lost jobs because of her previous role. Her career was nevertheless marked by great achievements. As one commentator noted: "She is one of the few women who made it past the bastions of male power in the 1930s and tried to instill her own brand of feminism into the labor movement."

FRANCES PERKINS

Other notable figures of the Depression era who struggled to improve working-class lives were not labor leaders but appointed or elected officials. Many of these political figures embraced social reform, but opted to work within the existing political system.

Frances Perkins (1882–1965) is most remembered as the first woman to hold a U.S. cabinet position. However, she had previously been both a suffragist and a settlement-house worker, and had also helped set up the special committee responsible for investigating the 1911 fire at the Triangle Shirtwaist Factory.

When Perkins served on the New York State Industrial Board, from 1923 to 1929, she came to the attention of Franklin D. Roosevelt, then governor of New York. In 1929 he appointed her state industrial commissioner and in 1933, just after he became president, made her secretary of labor. In that role, which she kept until Roosevelt's death in 1945, Perkins formulated New Deal labor policy, including the NRA and the 1938 Fair Labor Standards Act.

Frances Perkins made many enemies for her refusal to deport Harry Bridges; but although she was threatened with impeachment in 1939, she was able to retain her post. Her autobiography, *The Roosevelt I Knew* (1946), was the first account of the Roosevelt years to be published after his death. Perkins retired from government service in 1952 and died in 1965.

ROBERT F. WAGNER

Robert Ferdinand Wagner (1877–1953) was a German-born lawyer who was a vocal supporter of working people throughout his career (see boxes, page 70 and 91). Another New Yorker, he helped create much of the New Deal legislation relating to labor and relief. Wagner's first foray into labor issues was serving on the commission investigating the Triangle Shirtwaist Factory fire,

Eleanor Roosevelt

First Lady Eleanor Roosevelt occasionally worked closely with Secretary of Labor Frances Perkins. Together they set up camps across the United States where young unemployed women could participate in conservation and other projects. They were based on the Civilian Conservation Corps camps established for young men (see Volume 2, Chapter 5). Mrs. Roosevelt also worked alongside members of the Women's Trade Union League (see page 105). She believed strongly, as they did, that women employed in New Deal public works projects should receive exactly the same pay as men.

alongside Frances Perkins. The commission's efforts led to great improvements in New York working conditions.

On his election to the United States Senate in 1927 Wagner began to promote bills on a wide variety of issues, particularly those relating to unemployment. It was his idea to reduce joblessness by using people who needed work to staff public works projects. He also

•

"...one of the few women who made it past the bastions of male power..."

•

supported much major New Deal legislation, including the National Industrial Recovery Act (NIRA) and the National Labor Relations Act, also known as the Wagner Act. Wagner's considerable expertise on labor and labor economics distinguished him from many other legislators of his day.

Wagner was also concerned with many more issues, including health, public housing, and civil rights. He retired from the Senate in 1949 and died in 1953.

5. STRIKES AND VIOLENCE

One of the chief weapons in unions' struggle to improve their workers' lives was the strike, or the withdrawal of labor. The first strike in the United States, to oppose a pay cut, was held by New York City journeymen tailors in 1768. The first nationwide strike was called by railroad workers in 1877.

Until 1930s legislation gave unions the right to organize and strike, strikers frequently faced opposition from both employers, who often used physical intimidation, and the legal system. U.S. courts frequently ruled that strikes were illegal and issued injunctions to force strikers back to work. Strikers thus found themselves facing the police or national guard, as well as the private thugs, or "goons," hired by employers. In the desperate conditions of the Great Depression the situation was ripe for violence.

Rose Pesotta sits at her sewing machine in New York, 1944. The image publicized a book she had written about the labor movement.

SIT-DOWN STRIKES

Management used two common tactics against strikers. They might simply shut down a plant and refuse to negotiate, waiting for workers to give up; this was called a lockout. Or they might bring in scabs, the name strikers gave to strikebreakers brought in to do their jobs for less money. Often strikebreakers were drawn from the poorest parts of the workforce, such as immigrants or African Americans, whose desperation for work drove them to take any job offered.

Workers countered such tactics by creating the sit-down strike. During such actions they stopped working but remained in their places of work. Sit-down strikes proved a highly effective means of bringing many employers to the bargaining table.

had been laid off at the Goodyear Tire and Rubber Plant simply refused to leave the building. Within a month they had been given back their jobs by their shocked employers.

The General Motors' Strike

The sit-down strike technique was quickly adopted by automotive workers. The newly formed UAW staged its first sit-down strikes in 1936 to protest poor conditions,

the plant to be turned off and asked Flint police to seize any provisions brought to strikers. In one all-night skirmish police lobbed tear gas into the plant. The strikers retaliated with pipes and car parts, then chased their attackers away with spray from a fire hose. The police were defeated, and the strike carried on.

Governor Murphy then stepped in to restrain the police and prohibited General Motors from barring food deliveries. Finally, after a court-imposed deadline for workers to vacate the plant came and went, Roosevelt intervened. An agreement was finally reached on February 11, 1937, forcing General Motors to deal with the UAW.

The Strikes Spread

The UAW victory created a ripple effect throughout the country. By January 1937 sit-down strikes were underway in many other General Motors plants. Chrysler automotive workers conducted their own sit-down strikes in March 1937. Soon workers in other industries—store clerks, chefs, office workers, and utility company employees, as well as factory workers—began to take action. An estimated 400,000 Americans participated in such strikes in 1937; the total number of labor actions that year—work stoppages, strikes, and lockouts— was over 4,700.

Frances Perkins in 1938. Born in Boston, Perkins studied at both Pennsylvania and Columbia Universities before starting work.

One of the first sit-down strikes was held by employees of the Hormel Packing Company in 1933. The first sit-down strikes to gain a high profile, however, were staged in 1936 by rubber workers in Akron, Ohio. First, employees of the Firestone Rubber Plant prevented their management from implementing a wage cut and firing union workers through sit-down action. Then workers who

including work speed-ups, which, without proper safety mechanisms on heavy machinery, could result in serious injuries. The best known of these early automotive industry strikes took place at the General Motors Fisher Body Plant in Flint, Michigan. It lasted 44 days, from December 1936 to February 1937, in brutal winter weather. GM officials wanted to call in state troops to eject the workers from the facility, but state governor Frank Murphy refused, fearing that such action would cause serious violence. The corporation then ordered heat in

The Strikes End

In 1939 the Supreme Court ruled that sit-down strikes amounted to illegal seizures of property and so declared them unconstitutional. The strikes had had one lasting positive effect, however, in forcing large corporations to enter into collective-bargaining agreements with unions. Some corporations,

UAW members take it easy during the notorious 1936–1937 sit-down strike at General Motors Fisher Body Plant in Flint, Michigan.

like U.S. Steel in 1937, made this change without having been forced to by a sit-down strike.

THE USE OF VIOLENCE

Violence had been part and parcel of labor-management conflict in the United States since the advent of industrialization. Companies hired armed guards or used police or state militia to intimidate or attack pickets or other striking workers. Violence also often occurred when employers' forces escorted strikebreakers past strikers into places of work.

Violence against workers fit with a general attitude that saw them as replaceable commodities. Since management distanced themselves emotionally from employees, they would go to considerable and sometimes brutal lengths to prevent those employees from expressing their concerns about working conditions.

During the 1930s corporations adopted a policy for dealing with strikes known as the Mohawk Valley Formula. It involved the systematic attempt to rally public opinion behind the employers' cause. Typically, firms were eager to portray all labor leaders as highly dangerous radicals. Some firms even set up antilabor vigilante groups.

Violent Incidents

A particularly violent Depression-era strike was held by textile workers in Gastonia, North Carolina, in 1929. The strikers were defeated with so much violence that it horrified Americans. Two novels, *Strike!* by Mary Heaton Vorse, a noted labor journalist of

the day, and *To Make My Bread* by Grace Lumpkin, were based on the events. Another such violent incident, between UMW members and mine owners in Harlan County, Kentucky, in May 1931, resulted in an all-out gunfight that killed four people and injured more on both sides of the conflict.

Police, some on horseback, break up a crowd of longshoremen and others on the eve of the 1934 general strike in San Francisco.

Violence continued to mar labor actions in 1932. During a demonstration outside a Ford plant in Dearborn, Michigan, local police fired into the crowd. Four

A policeman wielding a nightstick attacks a striker in San Francisco in 1934.

people died, and more than 100 were injured. Later that year a strike by the Iowa Farmers' Union also descended into violence.

In 1934 mine owners bombed the homes of strike leaders in the Allegheny region of Pennsylvania with $17,000-worth of explosives. During the San Francisco general strike, called by the West Coast International Longshoremen's Association the same year, weapons used included baseball bats, bricks, and tear gas. Only intervention by the National Guard broke up the fighting.

In 1937 there was serious violence at Ford Motor Company's River Rouge plant. It was followed by a Memorial Day incident at a rally outside a Republic Steel plant in Chicago. An unarmed marcher threw a bottle or rock at police, who retaliated by brandishing nightsticks and opening fire on the crowd. Between 10 and 17 people were killed, about 80 were injured. Many were reportedly shot in the back. An inquiry judged the action to be "justified homicide."

Goons and Finks

The goons that employers hired to beat up and intimidate their workers sometimes included policemen or other law enforcement officers. Employers also paid informants to report to company management about union activity. Informants, usually company employees, were called "finks." The most blatant employer of such intimidatory tactics was the Ford Motor Company, whose founder, right-wing sympathizer Henry Ford, declared in 1937: "We'll never recognize the United Automobile Workers union."

Ford's River Rouge facility near Detroit had some 9,000 paid informants on a payroll of 90,000 and hidden microphones throughout the plant. Ford also employed some 800 "enforcers" to bully union organizers.

In May 1937 Ford's enforcers attacked a group of UAW organizers at River Rouge in an incident that became infamous as the Battle of the Overpass. UAW organizers, including union leader Walter Reuther, were standing on an overpass, distributing leaflets to workers. Ford's goons launched a

vicious physical assault on the union men.

In the four years following this incident Henry Ford came under pressure from the National Labor Relations Board to control his enforcers. Perhaps more influential was the reaction of his wife, Clara, who threatened to leave him if there were more bloodshed in his factories. He finally recognized the UAW in 1941.

This sort of thuggery was endemic to big industry. During an 18-month period General Motors spent about $1 million on private detective services to subvert labor activity. Companies such as the Pinkerton National Detective Agency, which supplied private security to corporations across the country, thrived. The agency is said to have made about $1.7 million between 1933 and 1936 for its services. Strikebreaker Pearl Bergoff, meanwhile, could provide corporations not only with men, but also an arsenal that included machine guns and tear gas.

Employers tried to justify the use of intimidation and violence. "We must do it to obtain the information we need in dealing with our employees," asserted Chrysler executive Herman. L. Weckler. In 1928 the chairman of the Pittsburgh Coal Company had told a Senate committee that his enforcers had machine guns "because you cannot run the mines without them."

Employers continued to use violent tactics throughout the Great Depression. These and many other civil liberties violations were investigated and publicized by the Senate's La Follette Committee, which sat from 1936 to 1940.

6. LEGISLATION

Much legislation enacted in the 1930s and 1940s was designed to improve conditions for workers. In part these laws were an attempt to stabilize the American economy by providing a framework in which financial recovery could occur. Resistance by corporations and conservative business leaders was frequent and vociferous.

NIRA

The first law to be enacted was the National Industrial Recovery Act (NIRA) in 1933. It contained labor-friendly provisions that laid down maximum working hours and minimum wages, provided

codes to ensure safe working conditions, and gave workers the right to organize unions. The first National Labor Relations Board was set up the same year to enforce collective-bargaining agreements, as provided for in the act.

Business initially supported government intervention but by 1934 it was clear that bureaucracy was making the laws effectively unworkable. Business leaders now saw the act as a threat to social stability. They came to believe that individuals within the National Recovery Administration (NRA) wanted to bring business under government or union control. Eventually, in May 1935 the Supreme Court declared NIRA unconstitutional (see Chapter 2, "The Supreme Court").

PROBUSINESS GROUPS

Probusiness forces formed organizations such as the American Liberty League to combat what was perceived as creeping government interference in private industry. Employers also started

Teamsters staged a major strike in Minneapolis in 1934. Two were killed in clashes with police. Fifty thousand people attended their funeral.

Goons and UAW members at Ford's River Rouge plant in 1937. The goons tried to stop the public seeing such images by stealing cameras.

to politicize groups such as the U.S. Chamber of Commerce and the National Association of Manufacturers (see Volume 5, Chapter 1, "Government, Industry, and Economic Policy"). The Association was anti-New Deal and anti-union. It supported open shops—workplaces where union membership was not obligatory—and

Labor Relations Act, also known as the Wagner Act, in July 1935. Roosevelt was lukewarm in his support, but the act was championed by Senator Robert F. Wagner, whose name it bears.

The Wagner Act contained many important provisions. In particular it gave unions the right to organize and made employers

Roosevelt's great contribution to the welfare of working people in the U.S. is commemorated in this New York mural, titled The New Deal.

legislation that maintained the status quo in industry. The only legislation it supported between 1933 and 1941 were bills to provide business subsidies.

THE NATIONAL LABOR RELATIONS ACT
Following the collapse of NIRA, Congress enacted more cogent labor laws under the National

enter into collective-bargaining agreements. The act also created a new National Labor Relations Board (NLRB), which continues to function today. This body is charged with oversight of any laws created under the act and with the enforcement of its provisions.

The constitutionality of the new act was challenged in 1937. This time around the Supreme Court affirmed its legality. Another important Supreme Court decision the same year declared that the new minimum wage applied to women as well as men.

The Taft-Hartley Act

The Taft-Hartley Act was passed in 1947. Its aim was to correct what a number of politicians perceived as the prolabor bias of the 1935 Wagner Act. The new act's provisions included the outlawing of closed shops, that is, workplaces in which only union members could be employed. It also gave the president power to demand an 80-day cooling-off period before strikes that might endanger national health or safety could take place.

THE FAIR LABOR STANDARDS ACT
The Fair Labor Standards Act, passed in June 1938, consolidated previous New Deal labor laws and limited working hours to 44 each week. Any additional hours now entitled workers to overtime pay. The act also established a national minimum wage of 25 cents per hour. This change led to raises for 12.5 million people nationwide. Other labor legislation passed in 1938 and into 1939 provided benefits for the unemployed. They included the food-stamp program.

THE NLRB AND THE UNIONS
The NLRB created under the Wagner Act was supportive of unionism, including the radical CIO. Its first members were prolabor and liberal, and more New Dealers joined as the board grew. In the belief that this was unfair, conservatives and AFL leaders lobbied for the inclusion of more

It's the American Way

OPPORTUNITY

FREEDOM OF Religion – Speech

PRIVATE ENTERPRISE

Representative DEMOCRACY

NAT... ...OCIATION OF MANUFACTURERS

ART RANDEL.

moderate board members, and two were appointed. Soon after the board began to favor the AFL. As a result Nathan Witt, the NLRB secretary, and his staff resigned in 1940. The NLRB continued to shape labor policy well into World War II, however and is still active today.

Subsequent legislation weakened the National Labor Relations Act. These laws included the Taft-Hartley Act of 1947 (see box, left) and a variety of amendments during the Republican administration of Ronald Reagan (1981–1989). Nevertheless, the National Labor Relations Act remains the foundation of U.S. labor law.

7. ASSESSMENT

The 1930s and 1940s saw an unprecedented expansion of American unionism. Unlike at any other time, legislative sentiment and public majority opinion coalesced against the interests of big business and in favor of labor. By the end of 1942 there were an estimated 11 million union members in the United States.

Establishing labor as a political and economic force was the result of the efforts not only of countless official organizers, but also of the many individual employees who participated in strikes and other actions of the CIO. The sense of empowerment that this gave working-class Americans provided them with a feeling of security and prepared them to take an active role in the economy and politics of modern America.

Many employers fought the rise in union power. But eventually the evidence forced them to acknowledge, however begrudgingly, that responsible unionism could help them, too.

The beliefs of the National Association of Manufacturers, which opposed unionization and supported "traditional" values, are made plain on this billboard, photographed in Iowa in 1944.

SEE ALSO

◆ Volume 1, Chapter 1, The United States, 1865–1914

◆ Volume 4, Chapter 1, Left vs. Right

◆ Volume 4, Chapter 2, The Supreme Court

◆ Volume 5, Chapter 2, Equality for Some

◆ Volume 5, Chapter 1, Government, Industry, and Economic Policy

GLOSSARY

balanced budget an economic term used to describe a situation in which a government's income is enough to pay for all its expenditure. The balanced budget was an essential principle in U.S. economic policy until Roosevelt adopted deficit spending in 1937. *See also* deficit spending.

business cycle an economic term used to describe the periodic but unpredictable and inexplicable rise and fall of economic activity.

capitalism an economic system in which private individuals and companies control the production and distribution of goods and services.

communism a political doctrine advocated by Karl Marx and Friedrich Engels in the 19th century that proposes the overthrow of capitalism and its replacement by working-class rule. Communism was the official ideology of the Soviet Union and was highly feared in the United States.

deficit spending an economic approach in which a government goes into debt in order to fund its activities. Deficit spending is a central tenet of Keynesianism.

depression a deep trough in the business cycle. No other depression matched the intensity of or lasted as long as the Great Depression.

fascism a political ideology based on authoritarian rule and suppression, aggressive nationalism, and militarism.

gold standard an economic tool that used gold as the measure of a nation's currency, so that one unit of currency always bought a fixed amount of gold. It was chiefly useful in stabilizing exchange rates between currencies.

Hundred Days the name given to Roosevelt's first period as president, from March 9 to June 16, 1933, characterized by a whirl of legislative activity. It was named for the Hundred Days of the 19th-century French emperor Napoleon.

individualism a political philosophy that argues that individuals are most effective when they are responsible only for their own well-being and not for that of other members of society.

installment buying a method of buying originally introduced by car companies in the 1920s that allowed purchasers to make a downpayment on a purchase and then pay the balance in a series of regular installments.

isolationism an approach adopted in the United States after World War I that argued that the country should disassociate itself from affairs elsewhere in the world. It led to the U.S. failure to join the League of Nations.

Keynesianism the economic theory advocated by John Maynard Keynes in the 1920s and 1930s. Keynes argued that governments should spend money to maintain full employment and stimulate the economy. His theories dominated most western democracies from the 1930s to around the 1980s.

labor union a formal organization in which workers act collectively in order to protect their interests such as pay and work conditions.

laissez-faire a French term for "let it be," used to describe an economy with no government regulation of business activity. Laissez-faire is an important part of classical or free-market economics, which holds that laws of supply and demand alone should regulate prices, wages, and other economic factors.

liberalism a political theory that emphasizes a belief in progress, the autonomy of individuals, and the protection of political and civil rights; also an economic theory based on competition and the free market.

mixed economy an economy that combines characteristics of a free-market economy—competition, private ownership—with a limited amount of state involvement, such as regulation of business, wage and hour legislation, and a degree of nationalization.

mutualism a U.S. political tradition that advocates cooperative action as a way to lessen the negative social effects of the economy. The mutualist tradition was behind the general acceptance in the 1930s that government had an obligation to look after its citizens.

nativism an anti-immigrant U.S. political tradition that values "real" Americans and their attitudes over those of more recent immigrants. In the late 19th century nativism saw first- or second-generation Irish immigrants objecting to newcomers from southern Europe, for example.

planned economy an economy in which economic activity is controlled by the state. Most businesses are nationalized rather than privately owned, and the government sets production quotas, wages, and prices.

populism a name given to numerous political movements of the 1930s that claimed to represent the common people; populism also describes the beliefs of the Populist Party formed in 1891 to represent rural interests and the breakup of monopolies.

progressivism a political tradition in the United States that advocated social reform by government legislation. Both the Republican and Democratic parties had progressive wings.

public works projects often large-scale projects run by federal, state, or local government in order to generate employment.

recession a severe decline in economic activity that lasts for at least six months

regulation a word used to describe moves by government or other agencies to control business activity, such as by legislation relating to minimum wages or maximum working hours or health and safety procedures.

relief the term most often used in the 1920s and 1930s for welfare.

Social Darwinism a social theory based on the theory of natural selection proposed by Charles Darwin. Social Darwinists believed that some people inevitably became richer or more powerful than others, and that inequality was therefore acceptable.

socialism a political doctrine that removes business from private ownership in favor of state or cooperative ownership in order to create a more equitable society.

welfare financial or other help distributed to people in need; the word is also sometimes used to apply to the agencies that distribute the aid.

FURTHER READING

Allen, Frederick Lewis. *Since Yesterday: The 1930s in America, September 3, 1929–September 3, 1939*. New York: HarperCollins, 1986.

Brogan, Hugh. *The Penguin History of the United States of America*. New York: Penguin Books, 1990.

Evans, Harold. *The American Century*. New York: Knopf, 1999.

Handlin, Oscar, and Lilian Handlin. *Liberty and Equality: 1920–1994*. New York: HarperCollins Publishers, 1994.

Jones, M. A. *The Limits of Liberty: American History 1607–1992*. New York: Oxford University Press, 1995.

Kennedy, David M. *Freedom From Fear: The American People in Depression and War, 1929–1945* (Oxford History of the United States). New York: Oxford University Press, 1999.

Meltzer, Milton. *Brother Can You Spare a Dime?: The Great Depression 1929–1933* New York: Facts on File, Inc., 1991.

Nardo, Don (ed.). *The Great Depression* (Opposing Viewpoints Digest). Greenhaven Press, 1998.

Parrish, Michael E. *Anxious Decades: America in Prosperity and Depression, 1920–1941*. New York: W. W. Norton & Company Inc., 1994.

Phillips, Cabell. *From the Crash to the Blitz: 1929-1939*. Bronx, NY: Fordham University Press, 2000.

Watkins, T. H. *The Great Depression: America in the 1930s*. Boston: Little Brown and Co, 1995.

Worster, Donald. *Dust Bowl: The Southern Plains in the 1930s*. New York: Oxford University Press, 1982

NOVELS AND EYEWITNESS ACCOUNTS

Agee, James, and Walker Evans. *Let Us Now Praise Famous Men*. Boston: Houghton Mifflin Co., 2000

Burg, David F. *The Great Depression: An Eyewitness History*. New York: Facts on File, Inc., 1996

Caldwell, Erskine. *God's Little Acre*. Athens, GA: University of Georgia Press, 1995.

Caldwell, Erskine, and Margaret Bourke-White. *You Have Seen Their Faces*. Athens, GA: University of Georgia Press, 1995.

Dos Passos, John. *U.S.A.* New York: Library of America, 1996.

Farell, James T. *Studs Lonigan: A Trilogy*. Urbana: University of Illinois Press, 1993.

Faulkner, William. *Absalom, Absalom!* Boston: McGraw Hill College Division, 1972.

Hemingway, Ernest. *To Have and Have Not*. New York: Scribner, 1996.

———. *For Whom the Bell Tolls*. New York: Scribner, 1995.

Le Sueur, Meridel. *Salute to Spring*. New York: International Publishers Co., Inc., 1977.

McElvaine, Robert S. *Down and Out in the Great Depression: Letters from the Forgotten Man*. Chapel Hill, NC: University of North Carolina Press, 1983.

Olsen, Tillie. *Yonnondio: From the Thirties*. New York: Delta, 1979.

Smedley, Agnes. *Daughter of Earth: A Novel*. New York: Feminist Press, 1987.

Steinbeck, John. *The Grapes of Wrath*. New York: Penguin USA, 1992.

———. *Of Mice and Men*. New York: Penguin USA, 1993.

Terkel, Studs. *Hard Times: An Oral History of the Great Depression*. New York: The New Press, 2000.

Wright, Richard. *Native Son*. New York: HarperCollins, 1989.

PROLOGUE TO THE DEPRESSION

Allen, Frederick Lewis. *Only Yesterday*. New York: Harper and Brothers, 1931.

Bordo, Michael D., Claudia Goldin, and Eugene N. White (eds.). *The Defining Moment: The Great Depression and the American Economy in the Twentieth Century*. Chicago: University of Chicago Press, 1998.

Cohen, Lizabeth. *Making a New Deal*. New York: Cambridge University Press, 1990.

Galbraith, John Kenneth. *The Great Crash 1929*. Boston: Houghton Mifflin Co., 1997.

Kennedy, David M. *Over Here: The First World War and American Society*. New York: Oxford University Press, 1980.

Knock, T. J. *To End All Wars: Woodrow Wilson and the Quest for a New World Order*. Princeton, NJ: Princeton University Press.

Levian, J. R. *Anatomy of a Crash, 1929*. Burlington, VT: Fraser Publishing Co., 1997.

Sobel, Robert. *The Great Bull Market: Wall Street in the 1920s*. New York: W. W. Norton & Company Inc., 1968.

———. *Panic on Wall Street*. New York: Macmillan, 1968.

Wilson, Joan Hoff. *Herbert Hoover: Forgotten Progressive*. Boston: Little, Brown, 1975.

FDR AND OTHER INDIVIDUALS

Alsop, Joseph. *FDR: 1882–1945*. New York: Gramercy, 1998.

Brinkley, Alan. *Voices of Protest: Huey Long, Father Coughlin, and the Great Depression*. New York: Knopf, 1982.

Cook, Blanche Wiesen. *Eleanor Roosevelt: A Life*. New York: Viking, 1992.

Fried, Albert, *FDR and His Enemies*. New York: St. Martin's Press, 1999.

Graham, Otis L., Jr., and Meghan Wander (eds.) *Franklin D. Roosevelt, His Life and Times: An Encyclopedic View*. Boston: G.K. Hall & Co, 1985.

Hunt, John Gabriel, and Greg Suriano (eds.). *The Essential Franklin Delano Roosevelt: FDR's Greatest Speeches, Fireside Chats, Messages, and Proclamations*. New York: Gramercy, 1998.

Maney, Patrick J. *The Roosevelt Presence: The Life and Legacy of FDR*. Berkeley: University of California Press, 1998.

Roosevelt, Eleanor. *The Autobiography of Eleanor Roosevelt*. New York: Da Capo Press, 2000.

Watkins, T. H. *Righteous Pilgrim: The Life and Times of Harold L. Ickes*. New York: Henry Holt, 1990.

White, Graham. *Harold Ickes of the New Deal: His Private Life and Public Career*. Cambridge, MA: Harvard University Press, 1985.

SOCIAL HISTORY

Clausen, John A. *American Lives: Looking Back at the Children of the Great Depression*. Berkeley, CA: University of California Press, 1995.

Elder, Glen H., Jr. *Children of the Great Depression*. New York: HarperCollins, 1998.

Gregory, James N. *American Exodus: The Dust Bowl Migration and Okie Culture in California*. New York: Oxford University Press, 1991.

Katz, Michael B. *In the Shadow of the Poorhouse: A Social History of Welfare in America*. New York: Basic Books, 1997.

Lowitt, Richard, and Maurine Beasley (eds.). *One Third of a Nation: Lorena Hickok Reports on the Great Depression*. Urbana: University of Illinois Press, 1981.

McGovern, James R. *And a Time for Hope: Americans and the Great Depression*. Westport, CT: Praeger Publishers, 2000.

Patterson, James T. *America's Struggle Against Poverty: 1900–1980*. Cambridge, MA: Harvard University Press, 1981.

Starr, Kevin. *Endangered Dreams: The Great Depression in California* (Americans and the California Dream). New York: Oxford University Press, 1996.

Ware, Susan. *Holding the Line: American Women in the 1930s.* Boston: Twayne, 1982.

Weiss, Nancy. *Farewell to the Party of Lincoln: Black Politics in the Age of FDR.* Princeton: Princeton University Press, 1983.

CULTURE AND THE ARTS

Benet's Reader's Encyclopedia of American Literature. New York: Harpercollins, 1996.

Davidson, Abraham A. *Early American Modernist Painting, 1910–1935.* New York: Da Capo Press, 1994.

Haskell, Barbara. *The American Century: Art & Culture, 1900–1950.* New York: W. W. Norton & Co., 1999.

Hughes, Robert. *American Visions: The Epic History of Art in America.* New York: Knopf, 1999.

McJimsey, George. *Harry Hopkins: Ally of the Poor and Defender of Democracy.* Cambridge, Mass.: Harvard University Press, 1987.

Meltzer, Milton. *Violins and Shovels: The WPA Arts Projects.* New York: Delacorte Press, 1976.

———. *Dorothea Lange: A Photographer's Life.* Syracuse, NY: Syracuse University Press, 2000.

Pells, R. H. *Radical Visions and American Dreams: Culture and Social Thought in the Depression Years.* Urbana: Illinios University Press, 1998.

Pollack, Howard. *Aaron Copland: The Life and Work of an Uncommon Man.* New York: Henry Holt & Co., Inc., 1999.

Thomson, David. *Rosebud: The Story of Orson Welles.* New York: Vintage Books, 1997.

Wilson, Edmond. *The American Earthquake: A Document of the 1920s and 1930s.* Garden City, NY: Doubleday, 1958.

INTERNATIONAL AFFAIRS

Bullock, Alan. *Hitler: A Study in Tyranny.* New York: Harper and Row, 1962.

Dallek, Robert. *Franklin D. Roosevelt and American Foreign Policy.* New York: Oxford University Press, 1979.

Kindleberger, Charles P. *The World in Depression, 1929–1939.* Berkeley: University of California Press, 1986.

Offner, A. A. *The Origins of the Second World War: American Foreign Policy and World Politics.* Melbourne, FL: Krieger Publishing Company, 1986.

Pauley, B. F. Hitler, *Stalin, and Mussolini: Totalitarianism in the Twentieth Century.* Wheeling, IL: Harlan Davidson, 1997.

Ridley, J. *Mussolini.* New York: St. Martin's Press, 1998.

WEB SITES

African American Odyssey: The Depression, The New Deal, and World War II
http://lcweb2.loc.gov/ammem/aaohtml/exhibit/aopart8.html

America from the Great Depression to World War II: Photographs from the FSA and OWI, 1935–1945
http://memory.loc.gov/ammem/fsowhome.html

The American Experience: Surviving the Dust Bowl
http://www.pbs.org/wgbh/amex/dustbowl

Biographical Directory of the United States Congress
http://bioguide.congress.gov

By the People, For the People: Posters from the WPA, 1936–1943
http://memory.loc.gov/ammem/wpaposters/wpahome.html

Federal Theater Project
http://memory.loc.gov/ammem/fedtp/fthome.html

Huey Long
http://www.lib.lsu.edu/special/long.html

The New Deal Network, Franklin and Eleanor Roosevelt Institute
http://newdeal.feri.org

New York Times Archives
http://www.nytimes.com

Presidents of the United States
http://www.ipl.org/ref/POTUS.html

The Scottsboro Boys
http://www.english.upenn.edu/~afilreis/88/scottsboro.html

Voices from the Dust Bowl: The Charles L. Todd and Robert Sonkin Migrant Worker Collection, 1940–1941
http://memory.loc.gov/ammem/afctshtml/tshome.html

WPA American Life Histories
http://lcweb2.loc.gov/ammem/wpaintro/wpahome.html

PICTURE CREDITS

TIMELINE OF THE DEPRESSION

1929
Hoover creates Farm Board
Stock-market crash (October)

1930
California begins voluntary repatriation of Mexicans and Mexican Americans
Smoot-Hawley Tariff Act
Little Caesar, first great gangster movie of the sound era
Ford cuts workforce by 70 percent (June)
Drought strikes Midwest (September)

1931
Credit Anstalt, Austrian bank, collapses (May 1)
All German banks close (July 13)
Britain abandons gold standard (September 21)

1932
Norris-La Guardia Act
Congress approves Reconstruction Finance Corporation (January 22)
FDR makes "forgotten man" radio broadcast (April 7)
Repression of Bonus Expeditionary Force by Douglas MacArthur (June 17)
Farmers' Holiday Association organizes a farmers' strike (August)
FDR wins a landslide victory in presidential election (November 8)

1933
Fiorello La Guardia elected mayor of New York City.
Nazi leader Adolf Hitler becomes chancellor of Germany
Assassination attempt on FDR by Giuseppe Zangara (February 15)
FDR takes oath as 32nd president of the United States (March 4)
National bank holiday (March 6)
Start of the Hundred Days: Emergency Banking Relief Act (March 9)
FDR delivers first "fireside chat" (March 12)
Economy Act (March 20)
Beer-Wine Revenue Act (March 22)
Civilian Conservation Corps Reforestation Relief Act (March 31)
Emergency Farm Mortgage Act (May)
Federal Emergency Relief Act (FERA) and Agricultural Adjustment Administration (AAA) created (May 12)
Tennessee Valley Authority (May 18)
Federal Securities Act (May 27)
London Economic Conference (June)
Home Owners Refinancing Act (June 13)
Banking Act; Farm Credit Act; Emergency Railroad Transportation Act; National Industrial Recovery Act;

Glass Steagall Banking Act (June 16)
73rd Congress adjourns (June 16)
FDR creates Civil Works Administration (November)

1934
U.S. joins International Labour Organization
Huey Long launches Share-Our-Wealth Society (January)
Farm Mortgage Refinancing Act (January 31)
Securities Exchange Act (June 6)
National Housing Act (June 28)

1935
Emergency Relief Appropriation Act (April 8)
Soil Conservation Act (April 27)
Resettlement Administration created (May 1)
Rural Electrification Administration created (May 11)
Sureme Court rules NIRA unconstitutional (May 27)
Works Progress Administration formed (May 6)
Federal Music Project introduced (July)
National Labor Relations (Wagner) Act (July 5)
Social Security Act (August 14)
Banking Act (August 23)
Public Utility Holding Company Act (August 28)
Farm Mortgage Moratorium Act (August 29)
Revenue Act of 1935 (August 30)
Wealth Tax Act (August 31)
Huey Long dies after assassination (September 10)

1936
FDR wins 1936 election (November 3)
Gone with the Wind published
Charlie Chaplin's *Modern Times* is last great silent movie
Supreme Court rules AAA unconstitutional (January 6)
Soil Conservation and Domestic Allotment Act (1936) (February 29)
Voodoo Macbeth opens in New York (April 14)

1937
Wagner-Steagall National Housing Act (September 1)
Supreme Court axes NLRB
CIO wins a six-week sit-down strike at General Motors plant in Flint, Michigan.
Supreme Court Retirement Act (March 1)
Bituminous Coal Act (April 26)
Neutrality Act of 1937 (May 1)
Farm Tenant Act (July 22)

Revenue Act of 1937 (August 26)
National Housing Act (September 1)
Start of sit-down strike at General Motors Fisher Body Plant in Flint, Michigan, which lasts 44 days (December)

1938
Amended Federal Housing Act (February 4)
Agricultural Adjustment Act (1938) (February 16)
Naval Expansion Act of 1938 (May 17)
Revenue Act of 1938 (May 28)
Food, Drink, and Cosmetic Act (June 24)
Fair Labor Standards Act (June 25)
Orson Welles' *The War of the Worlds* broadcast (October 30)

1939
John Steinbeck's *The Grapes of Wrath* published
Public Works Administration discontinued
Federal Loan Agency created
Supreme Court declares the sit-down strike illegal (February 27)
Administrative Reorganization Act of 1939 (April 3)
Hatch Act (August 2)
Outbreak of World War II in Europe (September 3)
Neutrality Act of 1939 (November 4)

1940
In California the Relief Appropriation Act is passed, raising the period of eligibility for relief from one to three years
Richard Wright's *Native Son* establishes him as the era's leading black author

1941
American Guide series published for the last time
Publication of James Agee and Walker Evans' *Let Us Now Praise Famous Men*
Japanese bomb Pearl Harbor, Hawaii, bringing U.S. into World War II (December 7)

1943
Government eliminates all WPA agencies

1944
Farm Security Administration closed

1945
FDR dies
Japanese surrender

INDEX